TWO SMALL ROOMS
...and a kitchen

A collection of recipes
from Queensland's
best known BYO restaurant

TWO SMALL ROOMS
...and a kitchen

Text by Michael Conrad and David Pugh
Foreword by Bob Hart
Photography by Peter Budd
Art Direction by George Trojanowski

Published by Two Small Rooms

Published in Australia by
Two Small Rooms
517 Milton Road Toowong Queensland 4066

Copyright Text © Michael Conrad and
David Pugh 1997

Copyright Photography © Peter Budd 1997

All rights reserved. Without limiting the
rights under copyright above, no part of this
publication may be reproduced, stored in or
introduced into a retrieval system, or
transmitted in any form or by any means
(electronic, mechanical, photocopying,
recording or otherwise), without prior
written permission of both the copyright
owner and the publisher.

National Library of Australia
Cataloguing-in-Publication data:

Conrad, Michael, 1964- .
Two Small Rooms...and a kitchen :
a collection of recipes from Queensland's
best known BYO restaurant.

Includes index.
ISBN 0 646 34074 3.

1. Two Small Rooms (Restaurant). 2. Cookery -
Queensland.

I. Pugh, David, 1957- . II. Budd, Peter, 1956- .
III. Two Small Rooms (Restaurant). IV. Title.
V. Title: 2 Small Rooms...and a kitchen.

641.509943

CONTENTS

Proudly produced entirely in Queensland,
Australia by the following:

Art Direction:
George Trojanowski

Design and Artwork:
Michelle Brown - The Studio
(a division of Delta Technology)

Pre-press and Colour Separations:
The Studio (a division of Delta Technology)

Printing:
Kingswood Press

6 - 7	FOREWORD
8 - 9	INTRODUCTION
10 - 13	LIST OF RECIPES
14 - 43	ASIAN
44 - 77	MEDITERRANEAN
78 - 111	MODERN CLASSICS
112 - 145	DESSERT
146 - 163	BASE RECIPES
164 - 167	GLOSSARY
168 - 171	INDEX
172	LIST OF RECIPE PHOTOGRAPHS
173 - 175	THANK - YOU

FOREWORD

It was eight years ago on a perfectly ordinary Sunday night that I sat down with two young men, a large and very good garlic souffle, and a decent bottle of shiraz. Or was it pinot noir?

Our objective: to add flesh to their carefully considered dream by arriving at a name for the restaurant they planned to open together. The two young men were Michael Conrad and Andrew Mirosch. Their restaurant was about to come to life in modest premises in Brisbane's Milton Road, and a serious decision about the name had to be made on that very night, if not sooner.

We tried everything. We worked through ingredients - coriander; aubergine; cassis; lemongrass; anise - in search of inspiration. We considered artists - Rembrandt; Matisse; Monet; Mondrian; Van Gogh; VAN GOGH? Composers? Star signs? Rock stars? World leaders? Fidel's, perhaps? Why not Joh's Bar & Grill? We even considered plagiarism. There was, after all, no Le Cirque in Brisbane. No Tour d'Argent, as far we knew. And no Moulin de Mougins. But no. So we opened a second bottle.

Place names, perhaps? Word games? Historic figures? Footy heroes? Fashion models? Race horses? How about Phar Lap's? More souffle anyone?

"How difficult can it be?" grumbled an impatient Andrew. "It's only two small rooms, after all."

"That's it," said Michael.

"What's it?" I asked.

"Two Small Rooms," said Michael.

"Perfect," said Andrew. "Now, can I have a beer?"

And so it came to pass that a restaurant, with an entrancing and thoroughly unpretentious name, was born. Sort of.

Andrew's food was distinctive, robust and stunning, Michael's presentation, polish and style were exemplary. The critics were entranced, the patrons beamed and spread the word. And from the day that it opened, Two Small Rooms looked, sounded, felt and tasted like a winner.

Two and a half years later, Andrew moved on to open "About Face" (a name he thought up all by himself). A year later David Pugh joined the team at Two Small Rooms. A new era blossomed from David's unique and fastidious approach. Even dizzier gastronomic heights were scaled, and national recognition increased.

The Queensland food revolution had begun with World Expo 88, but a year later, when Two Small Rooms opened, Brisbane was still struggling to find its culinary feet. Sydney and Melbourne were bounding into world contention, but Brisbane remained, somehow the poor, country cousin.

Two Small Rooms and many of the restaurants that arrived in its wake, have gradually but firmly changed all of that. Brisbane now offers food that can match anything in the south through the distinctive quality provided by the added freshness and intensity of ingredients that flourish within its immediate environment.

Recently, one of the most important and experienced of all Australian restaurant innovators - Melbourne's Mietta O'Donnell - called to tell me about a discovery she had made in Brisbane.

"We had the most remarkable meal up there, quite late at night, at a restaurant called Two Small Rooms," she said in her clipped, quiet way. "Have you heard of it?"

"The name rings a bell," I said. "Let me think ..."

Bob Hart - Melbourne - October, 1997

INTRODUCTION

Evolution is a constant theme at Two Small Rooms. Every dish presented, whether a new innovation or a classic revisited, is subject to the scrutiny and valued feedback of our staff and patrons alike before being dedicated to a place on our menu.

This process of evolution is driven by a philosophy of continual growth through learning and is steered by many influences. One such influence is the raw ingredients available to us. As the wealth of variety in quality produce grows, so too do the creative challenges and opportunities for our talented kitchen personnel.

However, the three main influences that have shaped Two Small Rooms are so stable and dominant, that our entire menu and subsequently the structure of this book are based around them. These are in fact geography, climate and history.

Opinions differ as to whether or not Australia is a part of south-east Asia. Whatever the answer, our geographic location has influenced our eating preferences enormously. Fragrant, spicy flavours not only lend themselves to our climate and lifestyles, but also to much of the local produce, both from the land and the sea.

Mediterranean flavours also form an important part of our restaurant's repertoire. It's not just that we share similar, warm, coastal climates, the rich, bold, flavours and textures of Mediterranean dishes are as exciting as any in the culinary world.

As fast as food changes, some dishes remain the same. The Modern Classics section is devoted to some of our personal favourites. Included are recipes ranging from delicate salads to the sumptuous decadence of Bordelaise sauce; foods that inspired many of us in our early days of cooking and still do. Our interpretations and refinements pay homage to these memorable dishes.

And what would a meal be without dessert? For at least ten and more likely fifteen years, I have heard people saying old-fashioned desserts are making a come-back. I think perhaps they never went away! Rich steamed puddings, custards, trifles and souffles are as "in vogue" now as they were in the late '70s when I first worked in the industry. Our collection offers many choices to provide the grand finale to a superb dinner party.

Lastly, the Base Recipes section offers a collection of recipes which appear often throughout the book as components of other dishes. From the complexity of a great stock-based sauce to the richness of your own ice cream, by using these recipes instead of packaged substitutes you will gain the rewards delivered by time and patience.

Every dish in this book is from a past or current menu at Two Small Rooms. Each photograph represents the food as it is served in the restaurant. The meals were prepared in the kitchen and immediately photographed in one of the "two small rooms". Peter the photographer and Frank, our waiter, took great delight in devouring all of the meals, as shooting proceeded, to make certain they tasted as good as they looked.

"Good produce" is the first rule when selecting a menu for an occasion. Always find out from your greengrocer or food store what is at its best and allow yourself to be swayed by what's available. Don't be afraid to have them order special things in for you. Better handling and storage facilities as well as prolonged seasons have increased the quality and variety of produce. Air freight allows us to have almost anything at any time of the year.

With the exception of the omelettes, all the recipes have been portioned for six people. All the methodologies have been carefully described for ease of use in the typical culinary enthusiast's home kitchen. Although not intended to be a text book, we believe the contents to be a practical guide to achieving professional results. We hope you find much pleasure both reading and cooking from "Two Small Rooms ... and a kitchen".

Michael Conrad & David Pugh - Brisbane - October, 1997

ASIAN

MEDITERRANEAN

MODERN CLASSICS

DESSERTS

LIST OF RECIPES

All recipes are portioned to serve six and in each section are ordered ranging from the lightest to the the richest flavours.

ASIAN

- SEAFOOD & LEMONGRASS BROTH : 17
- PEKING DUCK CONSOMME : 18
- THAI ROAST PUMPKIN SOUP : 19
- SALAD OF LEMONGRASS POACHED PRAWNS & COCONUT DRESSING : 20
- LEMON PEPPERED BEEF SALAD WITH CHILLI DRESSING : 22
- ASIAN SPICE CURED OCEAN TROUT : 24
- GRILLED TIGER PRAWNS WITH YELLOW CURRY DRESSING : 25
- SEARED SCALLOPS WITH CORN SALSA : 26
- JACK'S MUDCRAB OMELETTE : 28
- MORETON BAY BUGS WITH NAM PRIK SAUCE : 30
- SEARED CUTTLEFISH ON LINGUINE : 32
- MARINATED QUAIL ON VERMICELLI SALAD : 33
- GRILLED QUAIL ON YELLOW CURRY SAUCE WITH RAITA : 34
- SPICED SALMON FILLET WITH SOY & LIME BUTTER : 36
- STEAMED REEF FISH WITH FRAGRANT SPICES : 38
- FILLET OF BEEF WITH CHILLI & BLACK BEAN JUS : 39
- RED CURRY LAMB FILLETS : 40
- PEKING STYLE BARBECUED DUCK : 42

MEDITERRANEAN

- STEAMED ASPARAGUS WITH POACHED EGG & PARMESAN TOAST : 46
- MEDITERRANEAN GOAT'S CHEESE STACK : 48
- RISOTTO SALAD WITH CHICKEN TENDERLOINS : 50
- GAZPACHO WITH GARLIC BRUSCHETTA : 52
- NICOISE SALAD OF RARE TUNA : 53
- MOROCCAN SPICED CUTTLEFISH WITH FRUITY COUS COUS : 54
- SEARED SCALLOPS WITH WHITE TRUFFLE BUTTER : 56
- SCALLOPS & SQUID INK RISOTTO : 57
- CHAR-GRILLED ASPARAGUS ON TOMATO RISOTTO : 58
- BLACK LIP MUSSELS WITH SAFFRON RISOTTO : 60
- RISOTTO OF WILD & FIELD MUSHROOMS : 62
- MORETON BAY BUGS ON LINGUINE WITH HERB OIL : 64
- CALAMARI TOSSED WITH SPAGHETTINI & TAPENADE : 66
- CHERMOULAH CRUSTED SALMON : 67
- GNOCCHI & PRAWNS IN TOMATO SAUCE : 68
- SEARED CALVE'S LIVER ON BRAISED RADICCHIO : 70
- LAMB WITH NICOISE VEGETABLES : 72
- CHICKEN BREAST WITH BORLOTTI BEANS & TUSCAN SAUSAGE : 74
- BRAISED VEAL SHANKS WITH SOFT POLENTA : 76

MODERN CLASSICS

- FRESHLY SHUCKED OYSTERS WITH RED WINE VINEGAR DIPPING SAUCE : **80**
- ROAST GARLIC & BROWN ONION SOUP : **82**
- WILD & FIELD MUSHROOM BROTH : **83**
- ROCKET & COS SALAD WITH ANCHOVY MAYONNAISE : **84**
- FRESHWATER YABBIES WITH TRUFFLE & WALNUT OIL DRESSING : **86**
- OMELETTE OF WILD MUSHROOMS & BLACK TRUFFLE : **87**
- SCRAMBLED EGGS & SMOKED SALMON WITH CAVIAR : **88**
- TARTLET OF LAMB'S BRAINS ON ONION CONFIT : **90**
- SEARED VEAL KIDNEYS WITH BACON & SEEDED MUSTARD : **92**
- FILLETS OF REEF FISH WITH SAFFRON BEURRE BLANC : **94**
- ROAST GUINEA FOWL ON CREAMED CABBAGE : **95**
- BREAST OF CHICKEN WITH LEEK MOUSSELINE & MOREL MUSHROOMS : **96**
- SQUAB PIGEON WITH FOIE GRAS BUTTER : **98**
- MILK FED VEAL ON ROESTI WITH WILD MUSHROOMS : **100**
- RACK OF SUCKLING PORK WITH ROAST VEGETABLES : **102**
- LOIN OF LAMB WITH GARDEN PEAS & PARSNIP MASH : **104**
- FILLET OF BEEF WITH BORDELAISE SAUCE : **106**
- TRADITIONAL STEAK & KIDNEY PIE : **108**
- PEPPERED VENISON & BEETROOT RELISH : **109**
- RIB OF BEEF WITH BEARNAISE SAUCE : **110**

DESSERTS

- VANILLA BEAN CREME BRULEE WITH ARMAGNAC PRUNES : **114**
- WHITE CHOCOLATE BRULEE WITH RASPBERRIES : **116**
- LEMON SOUFFLE WITH LEMON MYRTLE ICE CREAM : **117**
- CHOCOLATE SOUFFLE WITH WHITE CHOCOLATE ICE CREAM : **118**
- DARK CHOCOLATE SORBET WITH BLACK CHERRIES : **120**
- PEACH & RASPBERRY TRIFLE : **121**
- RED WINE POACHED PEARS WITH RED WINE ICE CREAM : **122**
- MANGO TART & LIME CREAM : **124**
- BRANDY SNAPS WITH SUMMER BERRIES : **126**
- LEMON CREPES WITH BLACK SAMBUCCA ICE CREAM : **128**
- BITTER SWEET CHOCOLATE TART WITH CITRUS SALAD : **130**
- CHOCOLATE BROWNIE WITH ROAST COCONUT ICE CREAM : **132**
- APPLE & BANANA STACK : **134**
- BREAD & BUTTER CUSTARD : **136**
- DRUNKEN FRUIT STEAMED PUDDING : **138**
- SAUTERNE CAKE & SUMMER FRUITS : **140**
- HAZELNUT & ORANGE SABLE BISCUITS / BUTTER SHORT BREADS : **141**
- ALMOND ROCHERS / CHOCOLATE TRUFFLES : **142**
- CHEESE : **144**

ASIAN

Fragrant, spicy flavours that lend themselves to our lifestyles, climate and local produce.

SEAFOOD & LEMONGRASS BROTH

INGREDIENTS

1200 ml Chicken Stock
(see recipe page 148)

12 large Green Prawns
(shelled and de-veined)

6 Moreton Bay Bug Tails
(all shell removed)

12 Scallops

125 gm Cuttlefish
(trimmed and cut into strips)

2 stems Lemongrass

1 small knob Galangal Ginger
(peeled and finely sliced)

6 Kaffir Lime Leaves

1 stem Mint

2 Limes (juice only)

2 teasp Palm Sugar

2 Red Chillies (de-seeded and sliced)

50 gm White Fungus

50 gm Black Fungus

1 tblsp Fish Sauce

12 Coriander Leaves

METHOD

- Remove outside leaves from lemongrass.
- Slice bottom 8 cm thinly on a fine angle.
- Divide fungus and coriander between six bowls.
- Bring stock, sugar and spices to the boil in a large pot.
- Reduce to simmer, add prawns and bug tails.
- Allow to simmer for 2 mins.
- Add cuttlefish strips and scallops, cook for further 30 secs.
- Remove mint stalk and add lime juice.
- Divide between six bowls and serve.

PEKING DUCK CONSOMME

INGREDIENTS 2 litres Peking Duck Stock
(see recipe page 149)

300 gm lean Veal Mince

8 Egg Whites

1 desp Tomato Paste

1 Star Anise

8 Ice Cubes

2 desp Coconut Vinegar

GARNISH

12 Shitake Mushrooms

180 gm Peking Duck Meat
(cut into fine strips)

60 gm Black Fungus
(cut into fine strips)

60 gm White Fungus
(cut into fine strips)

12 Coriander Leaves

METHOD
- Mix all ingredients together in a stainless steel bowl.
- Place in a heavy pot, stirring frequently and bring to the boil.
- Remove scum from surface.
- Reduce to simmer and cook for 40 mins.
- Ladle soup out of pot gently and sieve through muslin.
- Serve very hot in deep bowls, pouring consomme over garnish.

NOTE When reducing heat after soup has first reached the boil, lower temperature slowly to keep raft floating on surface. Pak choy or choy sum leaves can also be added to make a more substantial soup. This soup makes for a great way to use left-overs when Peking Duck has been served at a dinner party. Clarified soup base can also be stored in an airtight container in freezer for future use.

THAI ROAST PUMPKIN SOUP

INGREDIENTS
- 1 large Butternut Pumpkin
- 2 tins Coconut Cream
- 6 Kaffir Lime Leaves
- 1 stem Vietnamese Mint
- 2 stems Lemongrass
- 1 teasp Prawn Paste
- 1 tblsp Sambal Oelek
- 500 ml Chicken Stock (see recipe page 148)
- 2 Limes (juice only)

METHOD
- Peel pumpkin and cut into small cubes.
- Roast in a hot oven until lightly browned.
- Pass through a mouli or mash until very fine.
- Add remaining ingredients except chicken stock and heat gently.
- Add chicken stock and stir until a smooth rich consistency is reached.
- Remove lime leaves, lemongrass stems and mint.
- Add lime juice and serve.

NOTE Grilled chicken tenderloins, green prawns or scallops make a good addition to this soup.

SALAD OF LEMONGRASS POACHED PRAWNS & COCONUT DRESSING

INGREDIENTS

24 large Green Prawns

2 litres Chicken Stock
(see recipe page 148)

4 stems Lemongrass

4 Kaffir Lime Leaves

75 gm Bamboo Shoots (julienned)

50 gm Pickled Ginger (julienned)

1/2 medium Salad Onion
(peeled and finely sliced)

18 Coriander Leaves

SALAD

100 gm Soba Noodles

1 medium Carrot
(peeled and julienned)

1/4 medium Daikon
(peeled and julienned)

1/2 Continental Cucumber
(peeled, de-seeded and julienned)

COCONUT DRESSING

1 tblsp Palm Sugar

250 ml Coconut Cream

3 Limes (juiced)

1 tblsp Fish Sauce

2 tblsp Nam Prik Sauce
(see recipe page 155)

METHOD

- Remove outside leaves from lemongrass, crush with the back of a knife and chop into three pieces.
- Bring stock, lemongrass and lime leaves to the boil in a large pot.
- Add prawns, remove pot from heat and allow to cool.
- Remove prawns from stock when cool enough to handle.
- Peel and de-vein prawns.
- Combine all salad ingredients in a large bowl, mix together and serve into six bowls.
- Lay prawns over salad.
- Combine all dressing ingredients until well mixed.
- Pour dressing liberally over salad and prawns, serve immediately.

NOTE   Whilst the dressing and salad need to be made immediately prior to serving, prawns can be pre-cooked earlier on the same day and all salad ingredients pre-cut and stored in refrigerator.

LEMON PEPPERED BEEF SALAD WITH CHILLI DRESSING

INGREDIENTS

450 gm Eye Fillet Steak
(fat and sinew removed)

1 bottle Sancho Pepper

2 Red Chillies
(de-seeded and finely sliced)

50 gm Bean Sprouts

SALAD

1 cob Sweet Corn

120 gm Green Beans

25 gm White Fungus
(torn into strips)

25 gm Black Fungus (julienned)

DRESSING

4 tblsp Nam Prik Sauce
(see recipe page 155)

1 tblsp Coconut Vinegar

75 ml Peanut Oil

75 ml Extra Virgin Olive Oil

METHOD

- Remove husk and strings from sweet corn.
- Sear whole cob in a hot pan until kernels are lightly coloured, remove and allow to cool.
- Remove ends and strings from beans.
- Bring a small pot of water to the boil, blanch beans for 30 secs.
- Refresh in iced water until cool, drain and slice on angle.
- Coat beef liberally in sancho pepper.
- Sear in a little peanut oil in a very hot, heavy pan.
- Seal all sides until lightly charred, reduce heat and allow to cook for 5 mins.
- Remove from pan and allow meat to rest for 10 mins.
- Slice meat thinly and arrange on six plates.
- Combine salad ingredients and arrange over beef.
- Whisk together all dressing ingredients.
- Spoon dressing over salad, season with sancho pepper and serve immediately.

NOTE

Salad ingredients can be pre-cut and stored in refrigerator. Dressing can be pre-made and stored in refrigerator. This salad can also be made with left-over roast meats.

ASIAN SPICE CURED OCEAN TROUT

INGREDIENTS

600 gm fillet Ocean Trout (de-boned with skin on)

100 gm Maldon Sea Salt (table salt can be substituted)

100 gm Brown Sugar

1 teasp Sichuan Pepper

1 teasp Dried Chilli (ground)

1 teasp Coriander Seed (ground)

1 teasp Lemongrass Powder

1 desp Pickled Ginger (very finely chopped)

1 desp Mint Leaves (very finely chopped)

1 desp Coriander Leaves (very finely chopped)

100 gm Mesclun Salad Mix (washed and dried)

100 ml Base Mayonnaise (see recipe page 153)

1/2 teasp Roasted Sesame Oil

1 Lemon (juice only)

1 teasp Fish Sauce

METHOD

- Combine salt, sugar, pepper, chilli, coriander seed, lemongrass, ginger, mint and coriander leaf in a stainless steel bowl (mix well).
- Lay fish on a large sheet of cling wrap and coat liberally with mixture.
- Wrap tightly and refrigerate for 24 hrs, skin side down on a flat tray.
- Remove from refrigerator, unwrap and scrape away marinade.
- Place on chopping board and dry with paper towels.
- Slice thinly like smoked salmon.
- Whisk together mayonnaise, sesame oil, lemon juice and fish sauce in a mixing bowl.
- Arrange sliced fish on six plates. Arrange salad leaves to one side of plates.
- Drizzle mayonnaise lightly over fish and salad. Serve immediately.

NOTE

Fish can be cured for shorter or longer periods for lighter or stronger flavours. Thinly sliced fish on crostini or cucumber will make a good canape for cocktail parties or pre-dinner savouries.

GRILLED TIGER PRAWNS WITH YELLOW CURRY DRESSING

INGREDIENTS 24 large Green Tiger Prawns (shelled and de-veined)

SALAD

1 small green Paw Paw

1 Salad Onion

1 Red Capsicum

1 Green Capsicum

2 Lebanese Cucumbers

12 Mint Leaves

12 Coriander Leaves

DRESSING

100 ml Yellow Curry Oil (see recipe page 154)

25 ml Coconut Vinegar

METHOD

- Peel, de-seed and julienne green paw paw.
- Peel and finely slice salad onion.
- De-seed and julienne red and green capsicums.
- Peel, de-seed and finely slice Lebanese cucumbers.
- Slice herbs finely.
- Combine all salad ingredients and mix well.
- Divide equally on to six plates.
- Saute prawns lightly in a teflon pan on medium heat (do not over-cook).
- Arrange prawns over salad.
- Whisk oil and vinegar together.
- Dress salad lightly and serve.

NOTE This recipe will work well with most fresh seafood. Barbecued seafood drizzled with a little curry oil while cooking and served with raita makes a great summer lunch.

SEARED SCALLOPS WITH CORN SALSA

INGREDIENTS

24 Coffin Bay Scallops
(or other scallop in shell)

2 cobs Sweet Corn

50 gm Green Beans

2 large Red Chillies
(de-seeded and finely chopped)

1 Red Capsicum
(de-seeded and finely chopped)

1 Salad Onion
(peeled and finely chopped)

50 ml White Wine Vinegar

75 ml Roasted Peanut Oil

1 Lime (zest only)

1/2 teasp Black Pepper
(cracked)

METHOD

- Remove leaves and string from sweet corn.
- Sear in a heavy pan on high heat until lightly brown.
- Remove from heat and allow to cool.
- Shave kernels from cob.
- Remove string and ends from beans.
- Blanch beans in boiling water for 1 min.
- Refresh in iced water, drain and cut into very small rounds.
- Mix together corn, beans, chillies, capsicum, onion, vinegar, oil, lime zest and pepper in a bowl.
- Cut scallop from shell with a small knife and remove hard muscle tissue.
- Blanch shells in boiling water for 5 mins, drain and allow to cool.
- Place a heaped teaspoon of salsa in each scallop shell.
- Arrange scallop shells on plates.
- Sear scallops in a heavy pan for 30 secs each side.
- Rest scallops on salsa and serve.

NOTE Some steamed rice or a small salad make a good accompaniment to this dish.

JACK'S MUDCRAB OMELETTE

(SERVES 4)

INGREDIENTS

OMELETTE

200 gm Mudcrab Meat (all shell removed)

100 ml Vegetable Oil

12 large Eggs (whisked)

1 pinch Salt

GARNISH

100 ml Nam Prik Sauce (see recipe page 155)

4 sprigs Coriander

STIR FRY

20 gm Pickled Ginger (cut into fine strips)

40 gm Bean Sprouts

4 Oyster Mushrooms (torn into fine strips)

1/2 Red Capsicum (julienned)

1/3 medium Carrot (peeled and julienned)

1/2 small Salad Onion (peeled and finely sliced)

40 gm Snow Pea Sprouts

20 ml Vegetable Oil

METHOD

- Heat vegetable oil for stir fry in a hot fry pan or wok and saute all ingredients very quickly.
- Spoon Nam Prik sauce over plates and divide stir fried vegetables.
- Heat omelette pan to medium heat, add 25 ml vegetable oil and pour in one quarter of egg mix (omelettes can only be made one at a time).
- Stir with fork and keep mix soft, place 50 gm crab meat in centre.
- Season to taste with salt and pepper.
- Fold omelette over and tap down on to garnished plate

NOTE

Some practice at making omelettes is advised before making this dish. Do not attempt this dish for larger groups as each omelette takes at least 2 mins to make. A partially broken omelette can be re-shaped by moulding between hands on the plate.

MORETON BAY BUGS WITH NAM PRIK SAUCE

INGREDIENTS 6 large green Moreton Bay Bugs

30 ml Peanut Oil

100 ml Nam Prik Sauce
(see recipe page 155)

12 Coriander Leaves

2 Limes (cut into wedges)

200 gm Jasmine Rice

6 Kaffir Lime Leaves

METHOD
- Split bugs in half with a large heavy knife.
- Remove intestines and rinse if necessary.
- Rinse rice under cold running water and drain.
- Bring 1 litre water and lime leaves to the boil in a medium sized pot.
- Add rice and boil, stirring occasionally until cooked (approx. 15 mins).
- Pour into a colander and rinse under hot running water.
- Remove lime leaves.
- Pre-heat grill to high.
- Brush bugs liberally with peanut oil, place under grill until cooked (8 mins).
- Spoon rice on to one side of plate.
- Rest bugs on rice and drizzle with nam prik sauce.
- Garnish with coriander leaves and lime wedges, serve immediately.

NOTE This dish can also be cooked on a hot barbecue.

SEARED CUTTLEFISH ON LINGUINE

INGREDIENTS
600 gm Cuttlefish
300 gm Linguine Pasta
30 ml Vegetable Oil
1 desp Salt

2 Limes (juice only)
2 desp Fish Sauce
1 desp Sambal Oelek
1 desp Palm Sugar

SAUCE
200 ml Coconut Milk
50 ml Peanut Oil
1/4 bunch Coriander
6 Sweet Basil Leaves

METHOD
- Remove skin from cuttlefish (if necessary) and score lightly in a criss-cross pattern on one side.
- Blend all sauce ingredients in a food processor on high speed for 3 mins.
- Bring 1.5 litres water, salt and oil to the boil in a large pot.
- Add pasta and cook until al dente (approx. 8 mins).
- Drain pasta in colander then divide into six bowls.
- Sear cuttlefish in a little vegetable oil in a very hot pan until lightly coloured (approx. 1 to 2 mins).
- Remove from pan and arrange over pasta.
- Pour sauce over cuttlefish and serve immediately.

MARINATED QUAIL ON VERMICELLI SALAD

INGREDIENTS 6 Quails (butterfly boned)

MARINADE

50 ml Lime Juice

50 ml Ketchap Manis

1/2 teasp Roasted Sesame Oil

100 ml Peanut Oil

2 Coriander Roots (finely chopped)

2 cloves Garlic (crushed)

1/2 teasp White Pepper

SALAD

150 gm Asian Vermicelli Noodles

1 cup Red Cabbage (finely shredded)

2 desp Pickled Ginger (finely sliced)

1/2 Salad Onion (finely sliced)

1/2 cup Pineapple (finely chopped)

75 gm Snow Pea Sprouts

GARNISH

50 gm Roasted Peanuts

METHOD
- Place quail in a shallow tray (skin side up).
- Mix all ingredients for marinade, pour over quail, cover with cling wrap and refrigerate for 6 hrs.
- Soak vermicelli in tepid water until soft (10 mins), remove from water and drain (noodles will still be quite elastic).
- Mix noodles with other salad ingredients.
- Remove quails from marinade and seal well on both sides in a heavy pan on moderate heat.
- Reduce heat slightly and add 1/2 remaining marinade, cover and cook for 5 mins.
- Divide salad between six plates.
- Remove quails from pan and place on salad.
- Pour remaining marinade from pan over quails, sprinkle plates with peanuts and serve.

NOTE When ordering quails, specify de-boned or butterfly boned. Chicken breasts can also be substituted in this dish.

GRILLED QUAIL ON YELLOW CURRY SAUCE WITH RAITA

INGREDIENTS
6 Quails (butterfly boned)

100 ml Yellow Curry Oil
(see recipe page 154)

12 sprigs Coriander

200 gm Jasmine Rice

6 Kaffir Lime Leaves

RAITA

100 gm Rockmelon
(peeled and diced)

100 gm Cucumber
(peeled and diced)

12 Mint Leaves (finely chopped)

1 clove Garlic (finely chopped)

1 desp Lemon Juice

200 ml Natural Yoghurt

YELLOW CURRY SAUCE

3 tblsp Yellow Curry Paste
(see recipe page 154)

200 ml Chicken Stock
(see recipe page 148)

450 ml Coconut Cream

METHOD
- Sweat curry paste in a heavy based pot on low heat for 10 mins.
- Add chicken stock and reduce by half.
- Add coconut cream, cook for 10 mins and strain.
- Rinse rice under cold running water and drain.
- Bring 1 litre water and lime leaves to the boil in a medium sized pot.
- Add rice and simmer, stirring occasionally until cooked (approx. 15mins).
- Pour into a colander and rinse under hot running water.
- Remove lime leaves.
- Brush quails with curry oil and char-grill or barbecue.
- Combine all ingredients for raita and spoon around plates.
- Serve rice in centre of plates and place quails on top.
- Spoon sauce around outside of plates, garnish with coriander and serve.

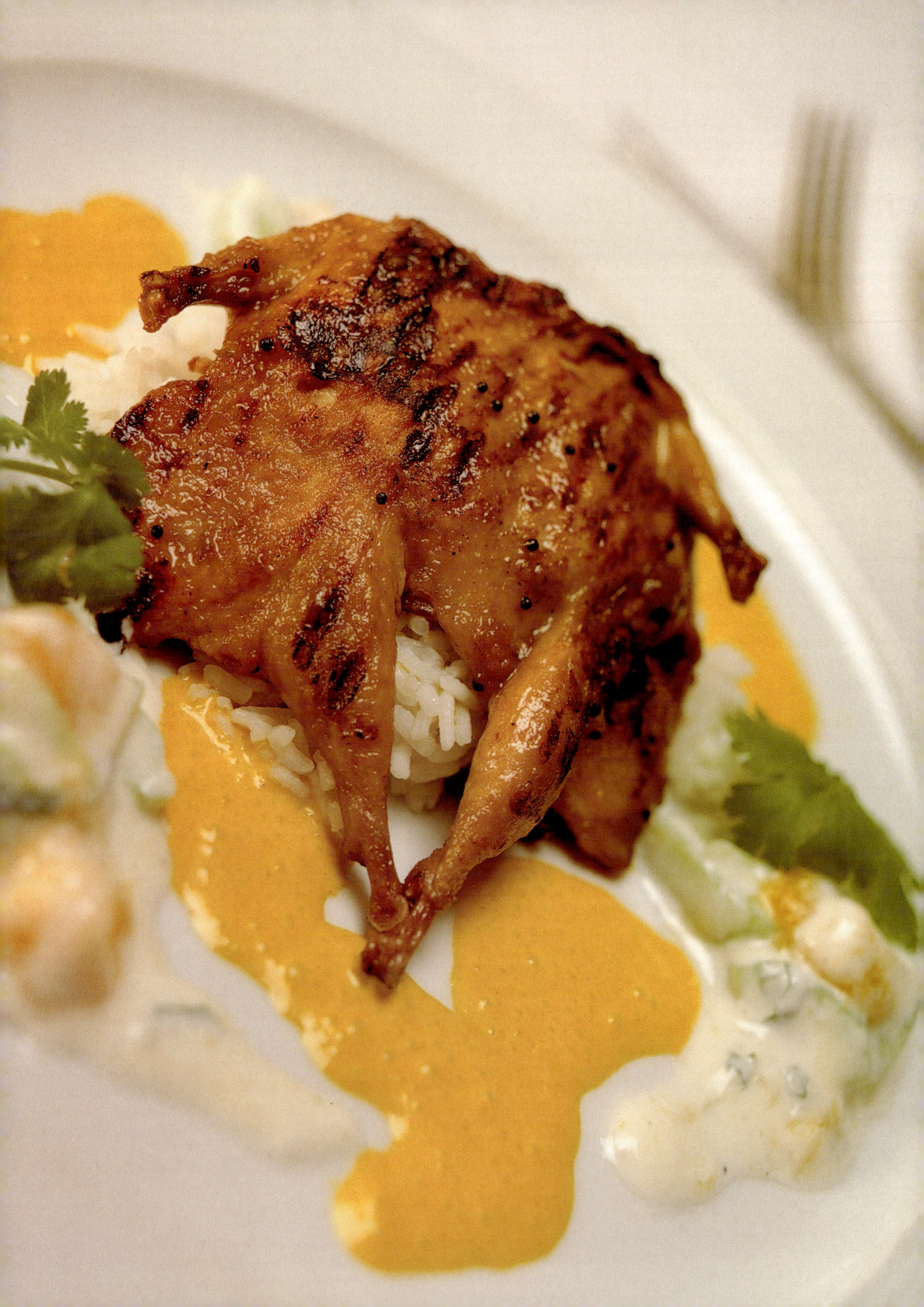

SPICED SALMON FILLET WITH SOY & LIME BUTTER

INGREDIENTS

6 x 150 gm fillets Atlantic Salmon (skin and bones removed)

1 teasp Hoisin Sauce

1 teasp Sambal Oelek

1 teasp Coriander Seed (ground)

1 teasp Sichuan Pepper

1 clove Garlic (finely chopped)

1 desp Peanut Oil

SAUCE

125 ml Coconut Vinegar

6 Shallots (finely sliced)

125 ml Chicken Stock (see recipe page 148)

50 ml Ketchap Manis

25 ml Cream

100 gm cold Unsalted Butter (cut into small pieces)

1 Lime (juice only)

4 Mint Leaves (chopped)

1 stem Coriander (chopped)

GARNISH

Potato Mash (see recipe page 157)

18 Baby Pak Choy (washed with outside leaves removed)

METHOD

- Combine all ingredients for marinade in a stainless steel bowl.
- Brush salmon liberally with marinade and allow to stand for 2 hrs in refrigerator.
- Reduce vinegar and shallots in a stainless steel pan on high heat until 1 desp liquid remains.
- Add stock and reduce by half, add ketchap manis and cream, return to the boil.
- Remove from heat and slowly whisk in butter, add mint and coriander.
- Allow to stand for 5 mins, add lime juice and strain.
- Grill salmon in a teflon pan on medium heat for 3 mins each side.
- Blanch pak choy in salted boiling water for 30 secs.
- Spoon potato mash onto plates and cover with pak choy.
- Rest salmon on pak choy, drizzle sauce around plates and serve.

NOTE

Atlantic salmon will dry out if overcooked and should be served medium-rare. Soy & lime butter sauce accompanies most seafoods as well as grilled meats

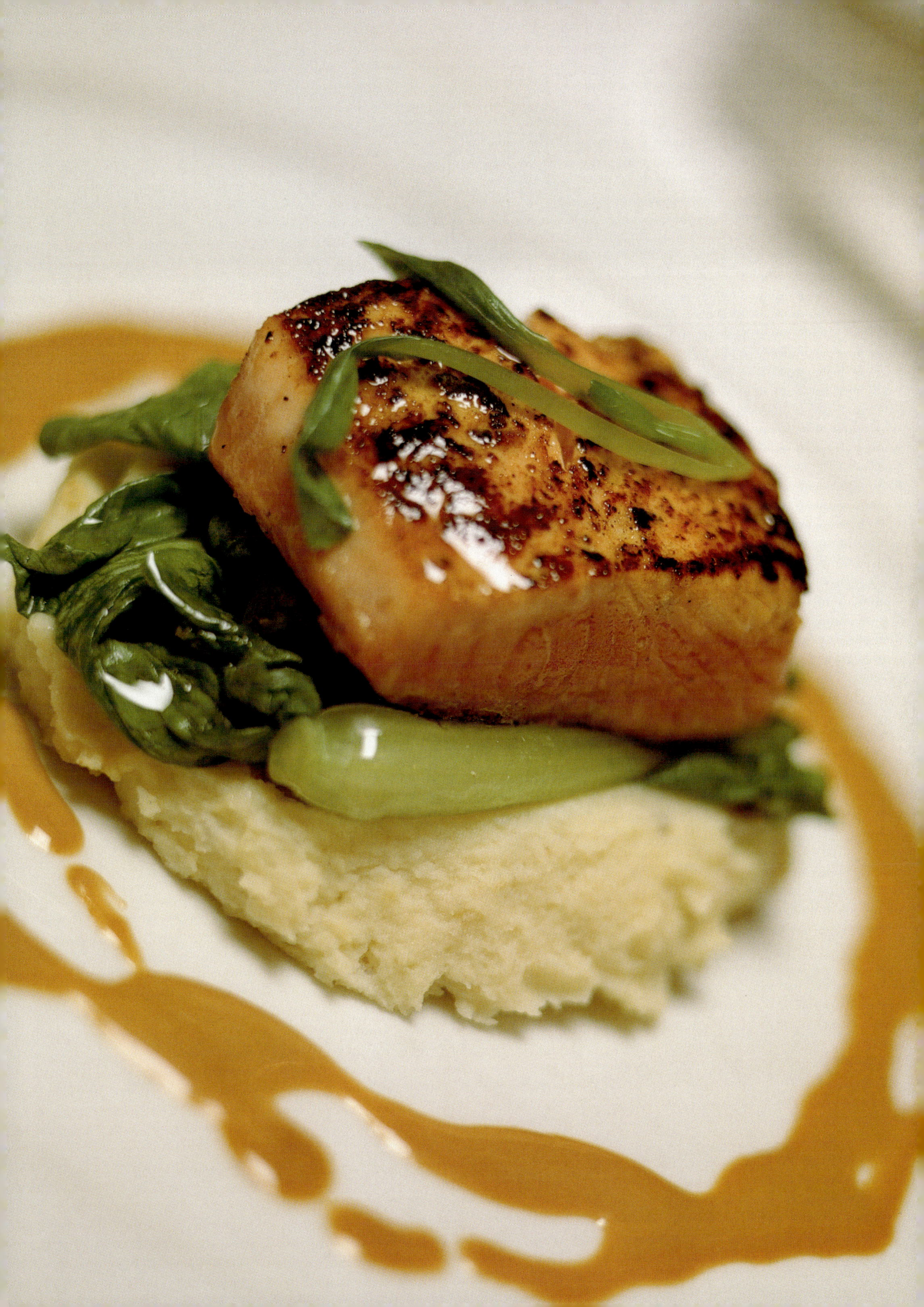

STEAMED REEF FISH WITH FRAGRANT SPICES

INGREDIENTS

6 x 150 gm Reef Fish Fillets (skin and bones removed)

1 teasp Garam Masala

1 teasp Cumin (ground)

1/4 bunch fresh Coriander

10 Mint Leaves

1/2 Lemon (zest and juice)

1 desp fresh Ginger (grated)

1 Brown Onion (finely chopped)

1 tblsp fresh Coconut (grated)

150 gm Unsalted Butter

1 desp Fish Sauce

GARNISH

400 gm Rice Noodles

3 fresh Limes (cut into wedges)

METHOD

- Combine herbs and spices in a food processor on high.
- Add fish sauce, onion, coconut, lemon and lastly butter, mix until smooth.
- Cut six large pieces of foil and butter.
- Rest each fillet on a piece of foil.
- Spread butter mix over each fillet and seal in foil.
- Place fillets in a large steamer and cook for 15 mins.
- Boil rice noodles for 5 mins in lightly salted water and drain.
- Arrange noodles in centre of plates.
- Remove fillets from foil and rest over noodles.
- Pour liquid from foil parcels over fish, garnish with limes and serve.

NOTE A whole fish (400 gm per person) can be cooked in this way. Place four deep cuts into the flesh of the fish and rub butter mix into cuts and stomach cavity. Make sure foil is well sealed and cook for 25 mins (approx. 10 mins per kilo).

FILLET OF BEEF WITH CHILLI & BLACK BEAN JUS

INGREDIENTS 6 x 150 gm Eye Fillet Steaks
(all fat and sinew removed)

SAUCE

500 ml Beef Jus
(see recipe page 150)

1 medium Red Chilli
(seeds removed and finely chopped)

2 desp Sweet Chilli Sauce

2 desp dried Black Beans

GARNISH

1 punnet Baby Corn

100 gm Sugar Snap Peas

1 bunch small Asparagus

100 gm Water Chestnuts (sliced)

100 gm Oyster Mushrooms

1 teasp fresh Ginger
(peeled and grated)

50 ml Peanut Oil

METHOD
- Soak black beans in cold water for 1/2 hr and drain.
- Bring beef jus and chilli sauce to the boil in a small heavy based pot.
- Reduce heat and simmer for 5 mins.
- Strain, add chopped chilli and black beans.
- Blanch baby corn in boiling water for 30 secs, remove and cut into thirds.
- Remove ends and any strings from sugar snap peas.
- Cut asparagus into bite size pieces and tear oyster mushrooms into strips.
- Seal fillet steaks until well coloured in a hot, heavy based pan (6 min each side).
- Remove from heat and rest in a warm place.
- Heat peanut oil in a wok until very hot.
- Stir fry corn, sugar snap peas, asparagus, chestnuts and mushrooms for 1 min.
- Add ginger, toss well and serve in centre of plates.
- Spoon sauce around outside of plates.
- Rest steak over vegetables and serve.

RED CURRY LAMB FILLETS

INGREDIENTS

12 Lamb Fillets (fat and sinew removed)
200 gm Jasmine Rice
4 Kaffir Lime Leaves
12 Coriander Leaves
120 ml Coconut Milk
1 Red Chilli (de-seeded and finely chopped)
1 desp Fish Sauce
100 ml Chicken Stock (see recipe page 148)
2 Limes (juice only)

RED CURRY PASTE

1 stem Lemongrass (roughly chopped)
1 teasp Garlic (finely chopped)
1 teasp Garam Masala
1 teasp Turmeric
1 teasp Cumin (ground)
2 teasp fresh Ginger (peeled and grated)
4 Cardamom Pods
1 Star Anise
4 Red Chillies
1 teasp Paprika
12 Black Peppercorns
1 desp Coriander (ground)
1 small Brown Onion (finely chopped)
100 ml Peanut Oil
2 Limes (zest only)

METHOD

- Blend all ingredients for red curry paste in a food processor until smooth.
- Brush lamb fillets with curry paste, cover and refrigerate overnight.
- Cook 1 1/2 tblsp curry paste for 3 mins on medium heat in a heavy based pot, then add coconut milk, chilli, 2 lime leaves, fish sauce and chicken stock.
- Bring to boil, reduce heat and simmer for 25 mins. Remove from heat, remove lime leaves and add lime juice.
- Rinse rice under cold running water and drain.
- Bring 1 litre water and 2 lime leaves to the boil in a medium sized pot, add rice and simmer, stirring occasionally until cooked (approx. 15 mins).
- Pour rice into a colander and rinse under hot running water. Remove lime leaves.
- On a pre-heated char-grill or barbecue, cook lamb fillets until well coloured on outside (4 mins), remove from heat and rest in a warm place.
- Serve rice in centre of plates, spoon curry sauce around outside of plates.
- Carve lamb, rest over rice, garnish with coriander and serve.

NOTE

This marinade also works well with poultry and seafoods. It will last well in refrigerator and is very handy for barbecues.

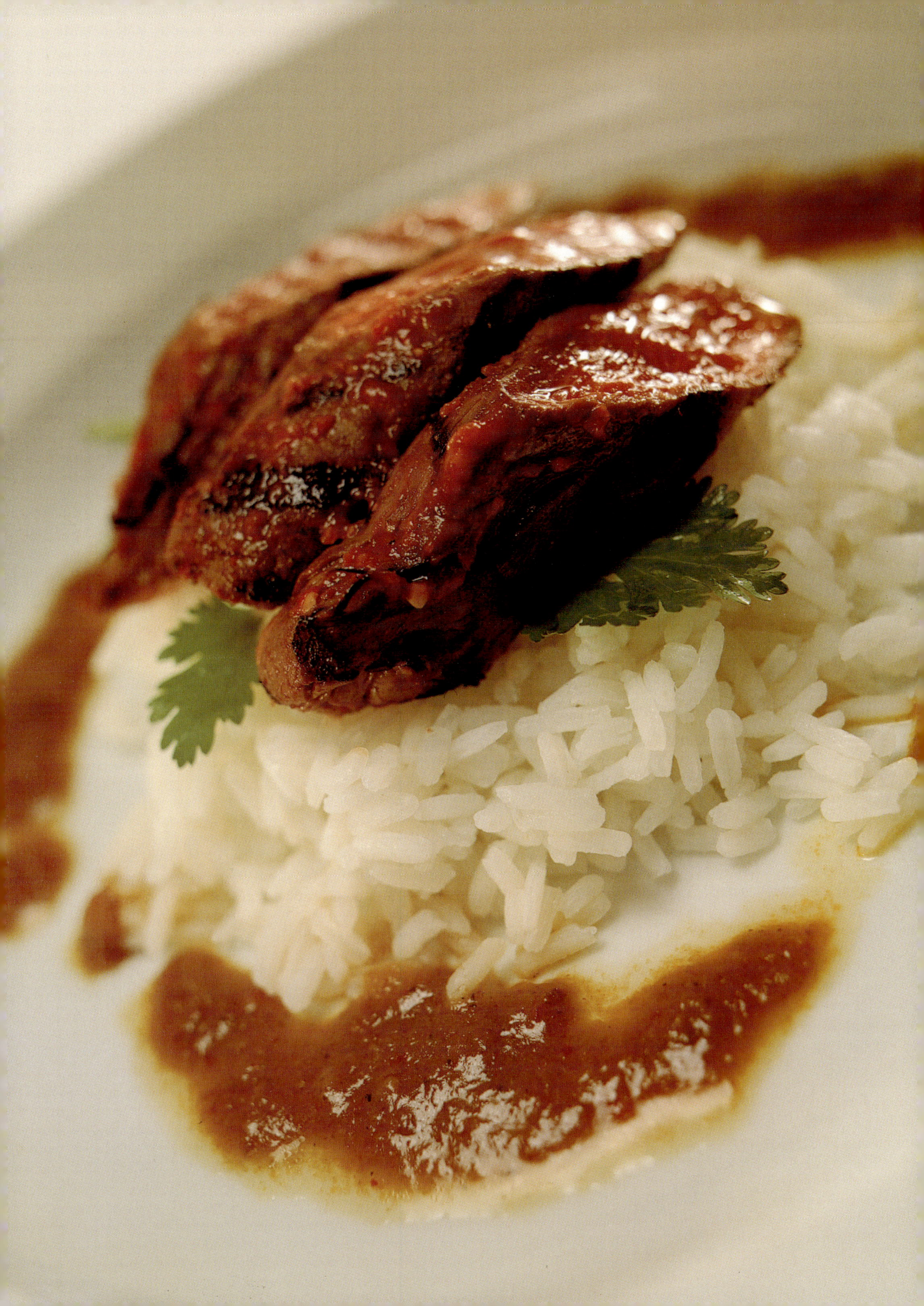

PEKING STYLE BARBECUED DUCK

INGREDIENTS 2 size 20 Ducks

MARINADE

1 teasp fresh Ginger (grated)

1 teasp Hoisin Sauce

1 teasp Five Spice

1 tblsp Honey

1 tblsp Soy Sauce

1 clove Garlic (finely chopped)

1/2 teasp Roasted Sesame Oil

1 tblsp Sherry (dry)

GARNISH

18 Baby Pak Choy (outside leaves removed)

18 Shitake Mushrooms

6 sprigs Coriander

1 medium Sweet Potato (peeled and sliced)

Capsicum Jam (see recipe page 158)

Peking Duck Sauce (see recipe page 151)

METHOD

- Wash ducks thoroughly under cold running water. Blanch ducks in boiling water for 3 mins.
- Hang ducks by neck over a tray for 1/2 hr to collect fat drippings.
- Combine all ingredients for marinade in a saucepan over low heat.
- Brush ducks inside and out with marinade and roast on a rack in baking dish with a small amount of water for 2 hrs at 170°C.
- After 45 mins brush ducks with marinade and cover loosely with foil.
- After 1 3/4 hrs remove foil and finish cooking.
- Roast sweet potato for 40 mins in an oiled baking tray, turning after 20 mins.
- Blanch pak choy in boiling water for 30 secs.
- Saute shitake mushrooms lightly in a little peanut oil in a hot pan.
- Arrange mushrooms around plates and pak choy in centre. Rest sweet potato on pak choy and spoon capsicum jam over sweet potato.
- Carve ducks and place on capsicum jam.
- Sauce lightly, garnish with coriander and serve.

NOTE

Obtaining great ducks can be very difficult and roasting them at home is very time consuming. For this dish, our recomendation is to buy your ducks already cooked from a barbecue shop in Chinatown. Buy cooked ducks on day of use and do not refrigerate before using.

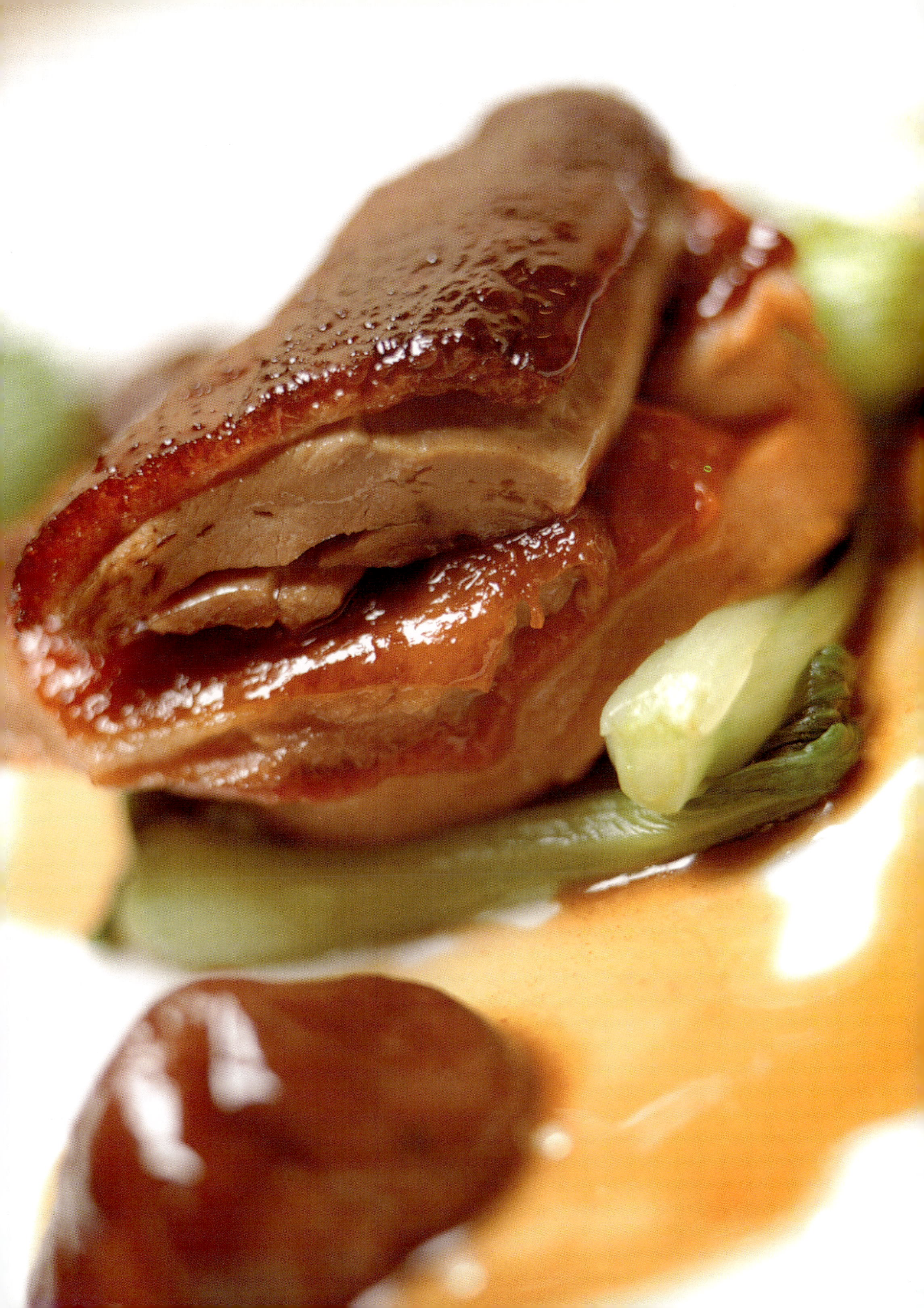

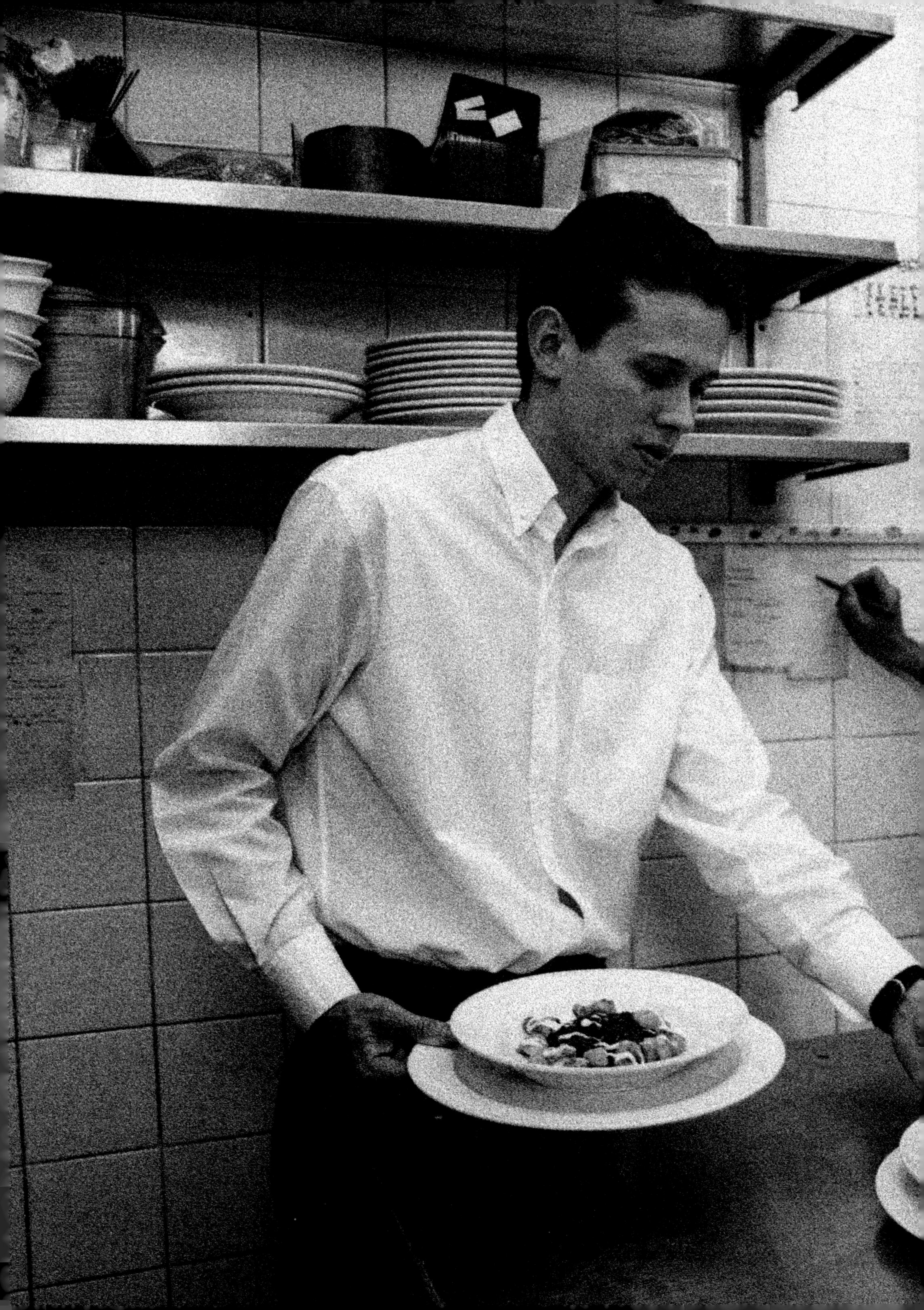

MEDITERRANEAN

Bold flavours and textures as exciting as any in the culinary world.

STEAMED ASPARAGUS WITH POACHED EGG & PARMESAN TOAST

INGREDIENTS

24 to 30 Asparagus Spears
(peeled and cut to same length)

100 gm Reggiano Parmesan
(shaved into large sheets)

6 slices Parmesan Brioche
(see recipe page 156)

6 Poached Eggs
(see recipe page 157)

1 teasp Chervil (chopped)

1 teasp Chives (chopped)

1 teasp Italian Parsley (chopped)

1 teasp Tarragon (chopped)

150 gm Unsalted Butter

METHOD

- Melt butter on low heat (do not colour).
- Stir in chopped herbs.
- Toast parmesan brioche lightly and place in centre of six warm dinner plates.
- Steam asparagus lightly over boiling water for 3 mins.
- Drain and place spears over toasted brioche.
- Rest poached egg on top of asparagus spears.
- Layer shaved parmesan over egg.
- Spoon butter sauce around outside of plate and serve.

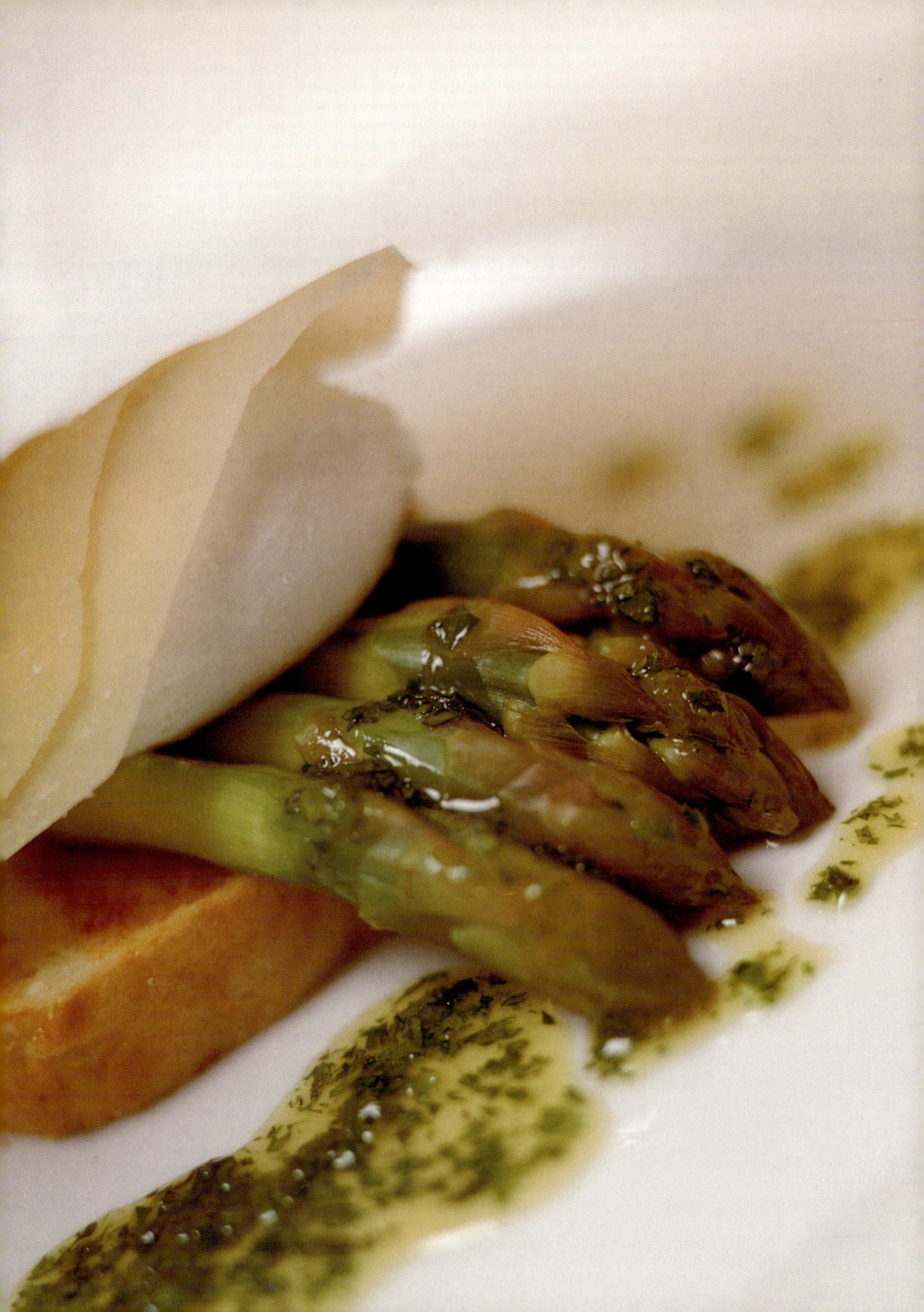

MEDITERRANEAN GOAT'S CHEESE STACK

INGREDIENTS

6 slices Olive Bread

300 gm Goat's Cheese (chevre)

1 1/2 Avocadoes
(6 thick round slices)

1 medium Eggplant

1 large Red Capsicum

2 medium Green Zucchinis

18 Kalamata Olives

60 ml Herb Oil
(see recipe page 153)

30 ml Balsamic Vinegar

Extra Virgin Olive Oil

18 sprigs Watercress

METHOD

- Slice goat's cheese into 6 pieces.
- Brush olive bread with olive oil and grill until lightly coloured.
- De-seed capsicum and cut into 6 pieces. Slice zucchinis thinly and slice eggplant.
- Sear capsicum, zucchinis and eggplant in olive oil on a char-grill or very hot pan.
- Rest eggplant on toast.
- Layer zucchini, capsicum and goat's cheese on a baking tray and warm gently in a moderate (160°C) oven for 3 mins.
- Place toast in the centre of plates and rest avocado slices on eggplant.
- Remove vegetable and cheese layers from oven and place on avocado.
- Scatter olives and watercress around outside of plate, drizzle with herb oil and vinegar, serve immediately.

NOTE

Olive toast can be substituted with sour dough or foccacia. Vegetable component of this dish can be prepared on previous day. An Australian farm-house chevre will work better than most French cheeses in this dish.

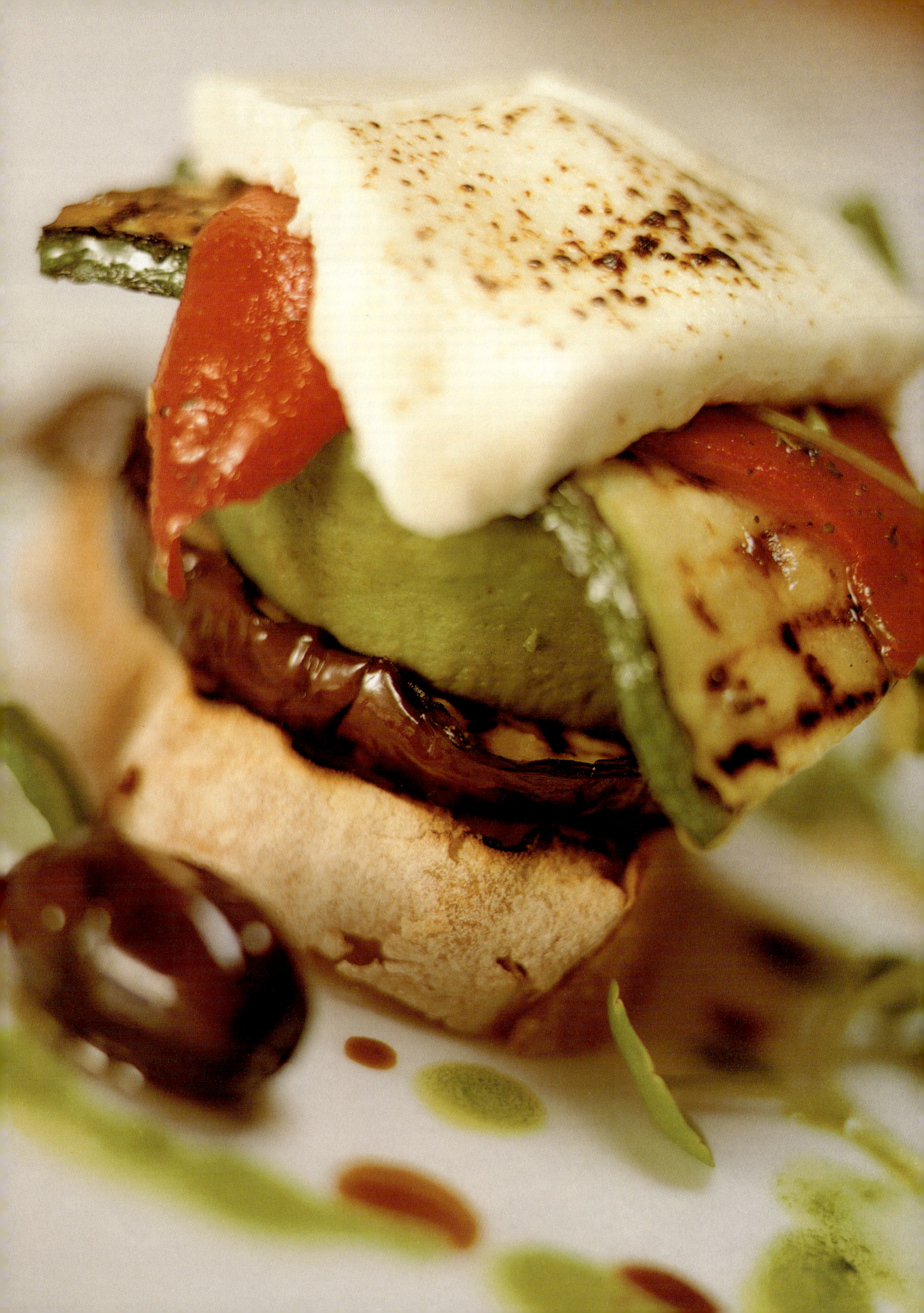

RISOTTO SALAD WITH CHICKEN TENDERLOINS

INGREDIENTS

100 gm Arborio Rice

500 ml Chicken Stock
(see recipe page 148)

1/2 Red Capsicum

2 small Green Zucchinis

30 gm Baby Capers

2 tblsp Italian Parsley
(finely chopped)

40 gm Sundried Tomatoes
(finely diced)

1 medium Salad Onion
(finely diced)

12 Chicken Tenderloins
(all fat and sinew removed)

Olive Oil

75 ml Herb Oil
(see recipe page 153)

18 sprigs Rocket

METHOD

- Saute rice in large pan in a small amount of olive oil until translucent.
- Add chicken stock and cook for 12 mins. Allow rice to cool in stock.
- Roast capsicums in a hot oven with olive oil until skin is blistered and starting to blacken. Cool, remove skin and seeds then finely dice.
- Cut zucchini into fine strips and lightly char-grill (or grill in a hot pan) in olive oil. Cool and dice finely.
- Mix capsicum and zucchini with rest of salad ingredients, season with black pepper and refrigerate in an airtight container.
- Arrange rocket leaves on six plates, place chilled rice salad in centre.
- Char-grill tenderloins lightly (or grill in a hot pan) in a little olive oil for 3 mins each side.
- Remove from heat, rest over rice, dress with herb oil and serve.

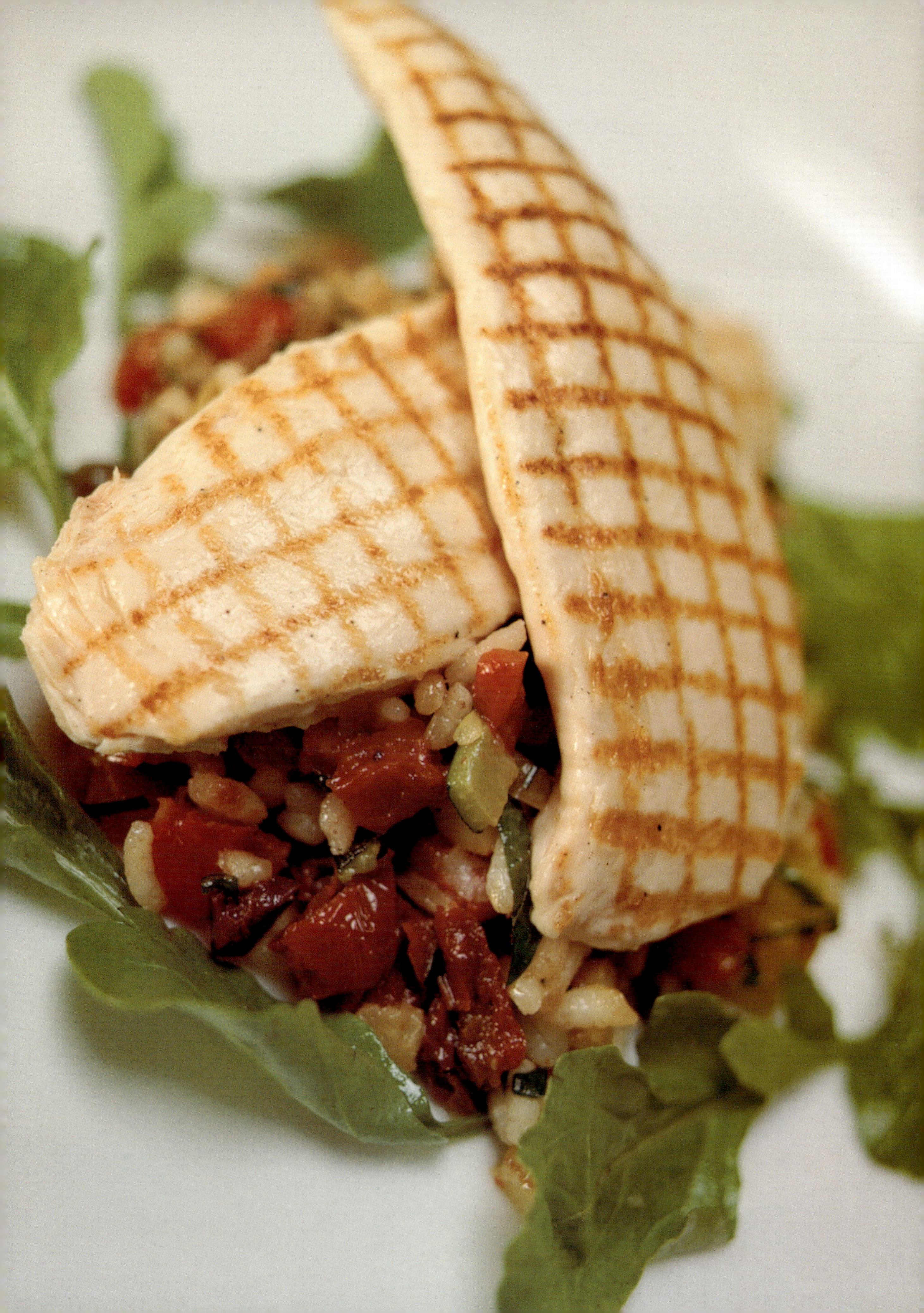

GAZPACHO WITH GARLIC BRUSCHETTA

INGREDIENTS

SOUP BASE

1.5 kg Roma Tomatoes

500 ml Chicken Stock
(see recipe page 148)

10 cloves Garlic

2 small Salad Onions (peeled)

1/3 cup Extra Virgin Olive Oil

1 Continental Cucumber
(peeled)

1 stick Celery

1/4 cup White Wine Vinegar

1/4 Fennel Bulb

SOUP GARNISH

6 Roma Tomatoes
(peeled, de-seeded and finely diced)

1 Egg (hard-boiled and grated)

1 small Salad Onion
(very finely diced)

1/3 Continental Cucumber
(peeled and very finely diced)

1/3 Green Capsicum
(very finely diced)

2 desp Italian Parsley (chopped)

1 teasp Black Pepper (ground)

BRUSCHETTA

2 Panini (sliced on angle)

1 clove Garlic (finely chopped)

1/2 cup Extra Virgin Olive Oil

METHOD

- Blend all ingredients for soup base in a food processor until smooth.
- Pass through a strainer and refrigerate until well chilled.
- Toast or grill panini, brush with olive oil and smear with garlic.
- Remove soup base from refrigerator and stir well.
- Half fill six bowls with soup base and divide garnish evenly between bowls.
- Serve with bruschetta on side plates.

NOTE

Fresh, cooked seafood added to this soup just before serving creates a wonderful summer lunch.

NICOISE SALAD OF RARE TUNA

INGREDIENTS SALAD

500 gm Tuna (cut into 1 cm cubes)

3 hard boiled Eggs (sliced)

100 gm Beanettes (blanched)

6 New Potatoes (boiled and sliced)

6 Anchovy Fillets

3 Roma Tomatoes (peeled and de-seeded)

24 Nicoise Olives

Black Pepper (cracked)

6 Cos Leaves (torn into strips)

2 slices Sour Dough Bread (crust removed and cut into cubes)

70 ml Olive Oil

DRESSING

30 ml Red Wine Vinegar

90 ml Extra Virgin Olive Oil

2 cloves Garlic (finely chopped)

METHOD
- Heat olive oil in a heavy pan and fry bread until lightly coloured.
- Drain and cool on kitchen paper.
- Sear tuna in a hot teflon pan for 1 min then remove from heat.
- Combine all salad ingredients in a large stainless steel bowl and mix gently.
- Divide evenly between six plates.
- Whisk dressing ingredients in a small bowl and dress salad liberally.
- Garnish with black pepper and serve.

NOTE Also works very well with Atlantic salmon.

MOROCCAN SPICED CUTTLEFISH WITH FRUITY COUS COUS

INGREDIENTS

450 gm Cuttlefish Meat (trimmed and lightly scored)

150 ml Base Mayonnaise (see recipe page 153)

2 desp Sambal Oelek

1/2 Lemon (juice only)

MARINADE

150 ml Vegetable Oil

1 teasp Cumin (ground)

1 teasp Coriander (ground)

1 teasp Caraway Seeds

2 teasp fresh Ginger (grated)

1 teasp Garam Masala

1 teasp Black Pepper

COUS COUS

200 gm Cous Cous

2 pinches Saffron Strands

1 teasp Turmeric

30 gm Dried Currants

1 Lime (juice and zest)

1 Preserved Lemon (rind only, finely chopped)

12 Mint Leaves (finely sliced)

1 medium Red Chilli (de-seeded and finely sliced)

200 ml Chicken Stock (see recipe page 148)

METHOD

- Combine all ingredients for marinade in a food processor, pour over cuttlefish and refrigerate for minimum 2 hrs.
- Mix together well, sambal oelek, mayonnaise and lemon juice.
- Bring chicken stock to the boil in a saucepan.
- Place cous cous, saffron, turmeric and currants in a ceramic bowl. Pour hot chicken stock over and stir well with a wooden spoon.
- Add lime juice and zest, preserved lemon, mint and chilli and mix well.
- Remove cuttlefish from marinade and sear on a hot grill until meat starts to colour (approx. 30 sec each side).
- Spoon cous cous into centre of plate. Rest cuttlefish over cous cous, spoon mayonnaise around plate and serve.

NOTE   Prawns, fish or chicken substitute well in this dish.

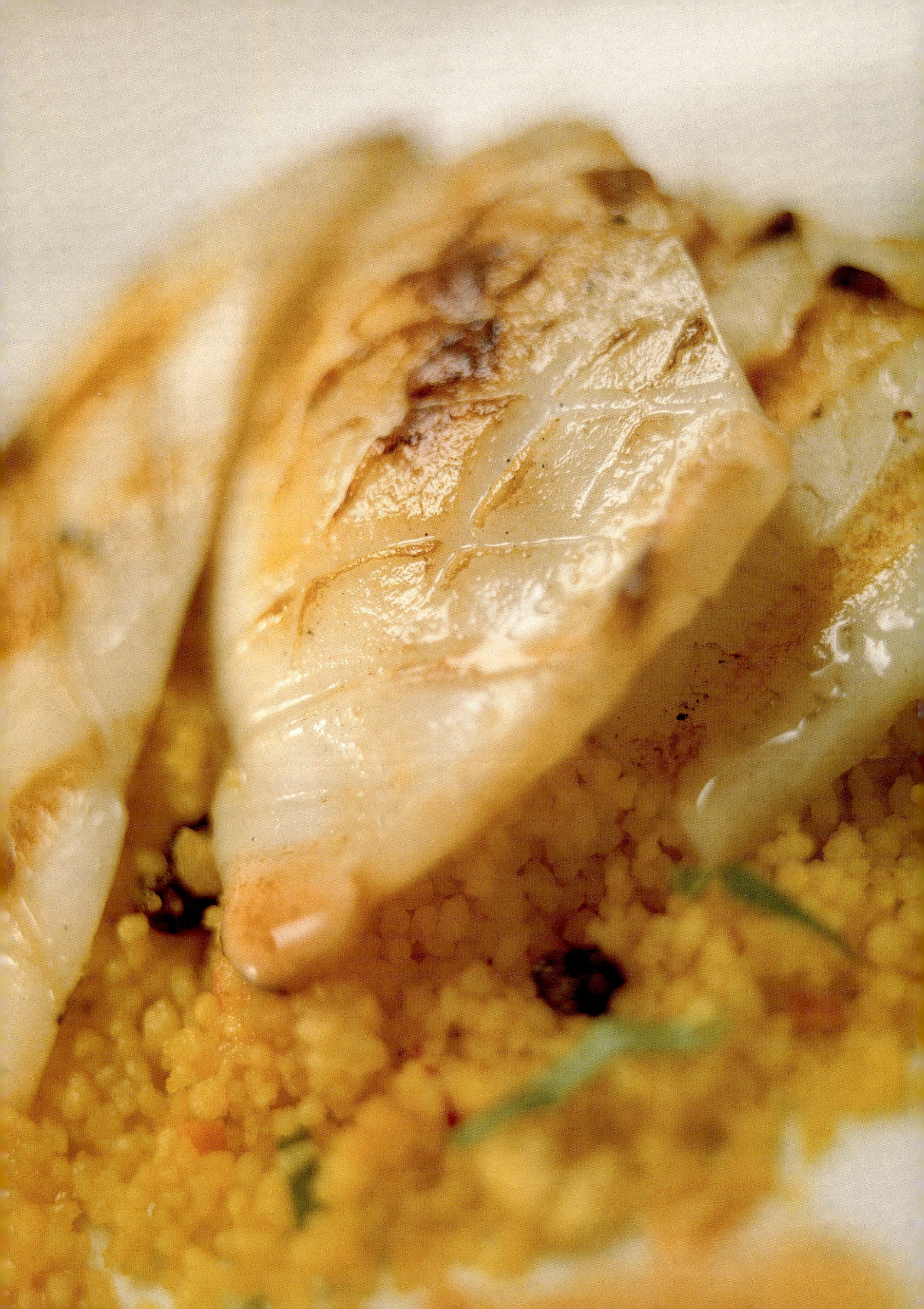

SEARED SCALLOPS WITH WHITE TRUFFLE BUTTER

INGREDIENTS

24 Scallops

200 gm Broad Beans

BUTTER SAUCE

40 gm Shallots (sliced)

750 ml White Wine Vinegar

6 Black Peppercorns

750 ml White Wine
(reisling or other unwooded wine)

250 gm Unsalted Butter (soft)

50 ml White Truffle Oil

1 teasp Lemon Juice

White Pepper (ground)

METHOD

- Bring shallots, vinegar, peppercorns and wine to the boil in a heavy pot, reduce by 7/8 (approx. 190 ml).
- Strain into a stainless steel bowl and slowly whisk in butter.
- Add truffle oil, lemon juice and season to taste.
- Shell broad beans and blanch in boiling water for 2 mins.
- Refresh under running water and remove skin from beans.
- Warm beans gently in a pot with a little butter.
- Sear scallops in a very hot teflon pan for 30 secs each side.
- Spoon broad beans on to one side of plate, arrange scallops around beans and serve sauce over scallops.

NOTE Fresh fettucine can be served as a garnish and to make this a more substantial appetiser. Other seafoods can successfully be substituted for scallops in this dish.

SCALLOPS & SQUID INK RISOTTO

INGREDIENTS

24 Scallops

RISOTTO

200 gm Arborio Rice

100 gm Butter (soft)

100 ml White Wine (reisling or other unwooded wine)

700 ml Chicken Stock (see recipe page 148)

150 gm Parmesan (grated)

2 tblsp Olive Oil

1 small Salad Onion (finely diced)

2 small Carrots (finely diced)

1/2 Leek (finely diced)

2 cloves Garlic (crushed)

20 gm Squid Ink

METHOD

- Heat olive oil in heavy based pot on high heat and sweat onion, carrot and leek until soft (3 to 5 mins).
- Add arborio rice and cook until translucent (1 min).
- Add white wine and reduce, stirring constantly.
- Add chicken stock until rice is just covered and simmer for 15 mins.
- Add butter slowly as well as garlic, squid ink and parmesan.
- Divide between six bowls when all ingredients are well amalgamated and desired consistency is reached.
- Sear scallops in a very hot teflon pan for 30 sec each side and rest over risotto. Pour any pan juices over risotto and serve.

CHAR-GRILLED ASPARAGUS ON TOMATO RISOTTO

INGREDIENTS

24 large Asparagus Spears (peeled)

50 ml Sherry Vinegar

RISOTTO

200 gm Arborio Rice

100 gm Butter (soft)

100 ml Tomato Juice

1 desp Tomato Paste

6 Roma Tomatoes (de-seeded and diced)

700 ml Chicken Stock (see recipe page 148)

150 gm Parmesan (grated)

2 tblsp Olive Oil

1 small Salad Onion (finely diced)

1 small Carrot (finely diced)

1/2 Leek (finely diced)

2 cloves Garlic (crushed)

METHOD

- Heat olive oil in heavy based pot on high heat and sweat onion, carrot and leek until soft (3 to 5 mins).
- Add arborio rice and cook until translucent (1 min).
- Add tomato paste and juice and cook for 5 mins.
- Add chicken stock until rice is just covered and simmer for 12 mins.
- Add butter slowly as well as garlic, parmesan and diced tomato.
- Divide between six bowls when all ingredients are well amalgamated and desired consistency is reached.
- Bring a large pot of water to the boil and blanch asparagus for 1 min.
- On a char-grill or hot pan, cook asparagus until lightly coloured.
- Rest asparagus over risotto, sprinkle lightly with vinegar and serve.

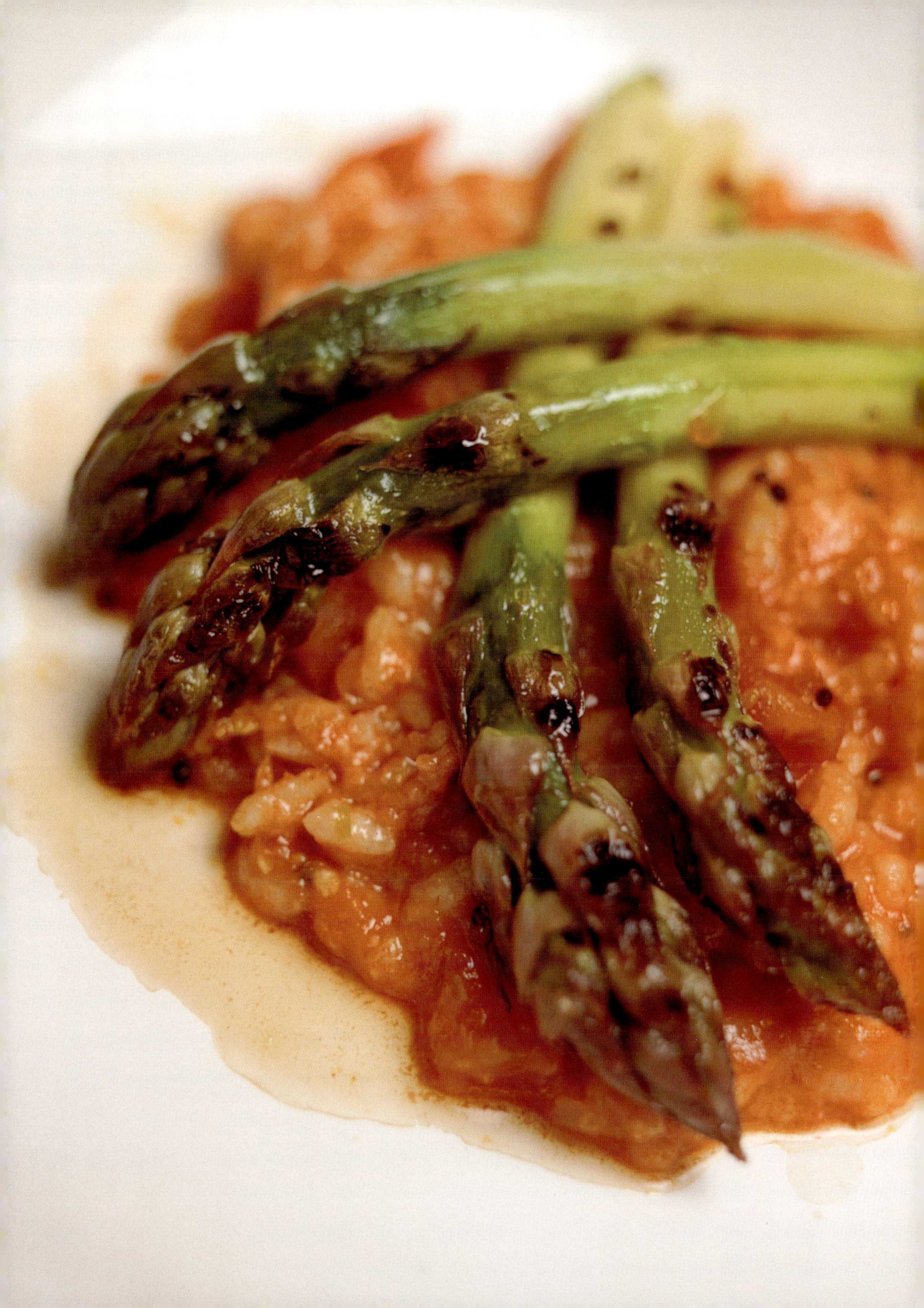

BLACK LIP MUSSELS WITH SAFFRON RISOTTO

INGREDIENTS

36 Black Lip Mussels (scrubbed)

50 ml White Wine (riesling or other unwooded wine)

30 ml Vegetable Oil

RISOTTO

200 gm Arborio Rice

100 gm Butter (soft)

100 ml White Wine (riesling or other unwooded wine)

2 pinches Saffron Strands

650 ml Chicken Stock (see recipe page 148)

150 gm Parmesan (grated)

2 tblsp Olive Oil

1 small Salad Onion (finely diced)

1 small Carrot (finely diced)

1/2 Leek (finely diced)

2 cloves Garlic (crushed)

3 Roma Tomatoes (de-seeded and diced)

2 desp Italian Parsley (chopped)

METHOD

- Heat oil in a heavy based pan on high heat.
- Add mussels and white wine, cook until shells start to open, remove from heat. Reserve liquid and mussels separately.
- Heat olive oil in heavy based pot on high heat and sweat onion, carrot and leek until soft (3 to 5 mins).
- Add arborio rice and cook until translucent (1 min).
- Add white wine and saffron, reduce stirring constantly.
- Add chicken stock until rice is just covered and simmer for 15 mins.
- Add butter slowly as well as garlic, parmesan, tomato, parsley and reserved juice from mussels.
- Add mussels when all ingredients are well amalgamated and desired consistency is reached, divide between six bowls and serve.

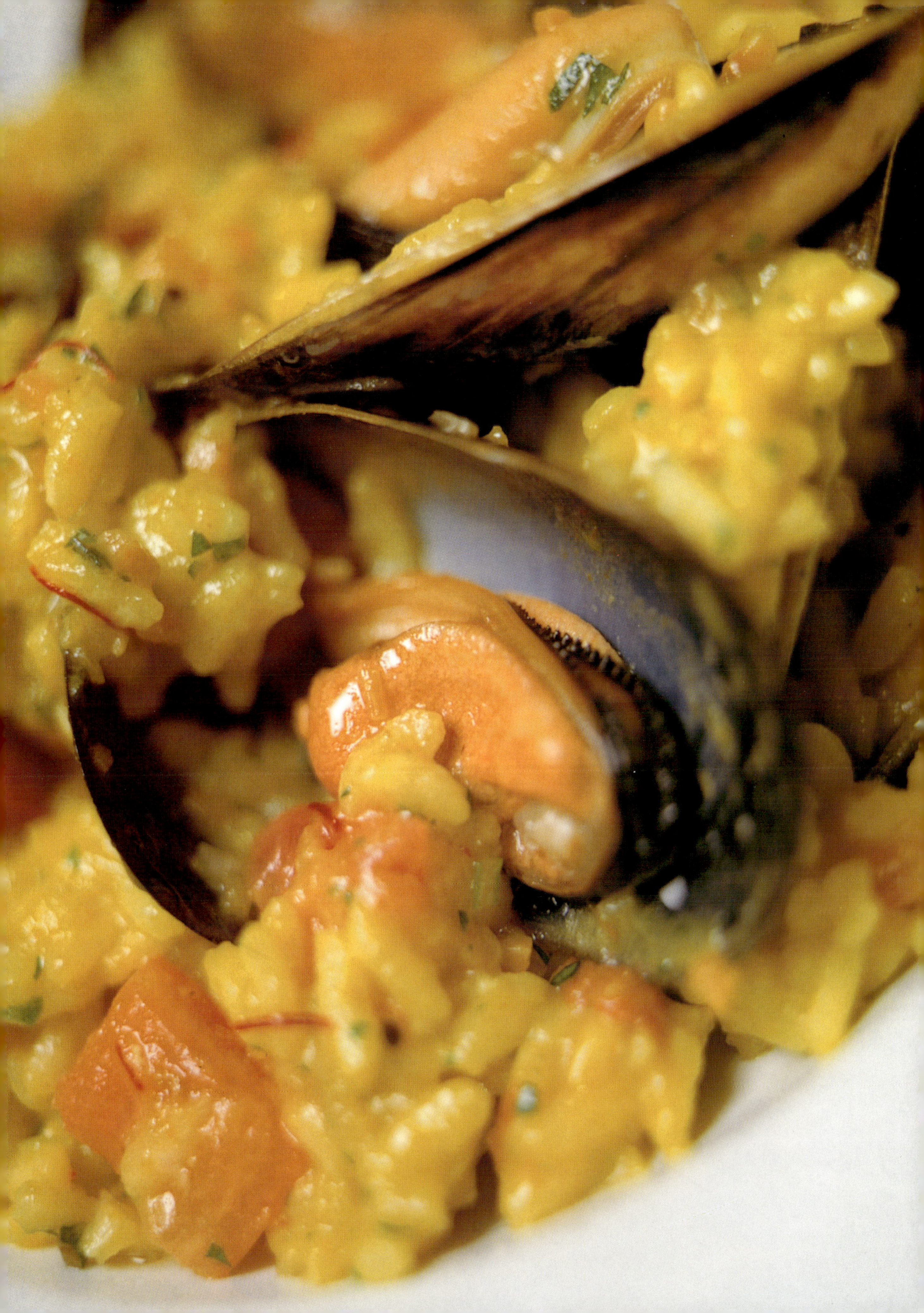

RISOTTO OF WILD & FIELD MUSHROOMS

INGREDIENTS

200 gm Arborio Rice

100 gm Butter (soft)

100 ml White Wine (riesling or other unwooded wine)

700 ml Chicken Stock (see page 148)

150 gm Parmesan (grated)

Olive Oil

1 small Salad Onion (finely diced)

1 small Carrot (finely diced)

1/2 Leek (finely diced)

2 cloves Garlic (crushed)

50 gm White Fungus (cut into small pieces)

50 gm Black Fungus (cut into strips)

100 gm Shitake Mushrooms (cut into quarters)

100 gm Oyster Mushrooms (cut into strips)

100 gm Pine Mushrooms (sliced)

2 Shallots (sliced)

GARNISH

Chervil (leaves only)

METHOD

- Heat 4 tblsp olive oil in a heavy based pan on high heat and saute mushrooms, one variety at a time. Remove from heat, reserve liquid and mushrooms separately.
- Heat 1/2 tblsp olive oil and saute shallots. Reserve liquid separately.
- Heat 2 tblsp olive oil in heavy based pot on high heat and sweat onion, carrot and leek until soft (3 to 5 mins).
- Add arborio rice and cook until translucent (1 min).
- Add white wine and reduce stirring constantly.
- Add chicken stock until rice is just covered and simmer for 15 mins.
- Add butter slowly as well as garlic, parmesan and reserved juice from mushrooms and shallots.
- Divide between six bowls when all ingredients are well amalgamated and desired consistency is reached.
- Mix mushrooms and shallots together and warm through in oven, or lightly saute and serve over rice.

NOTE

Unavailable mushrooms should be substituted with field mushrooms. A few drops of truffle, porcini or rosemary oil drizzled over this dish will enhance all the flavours. As well as a great dish on its own this can make an excellent accompaniment to roast veal or game.

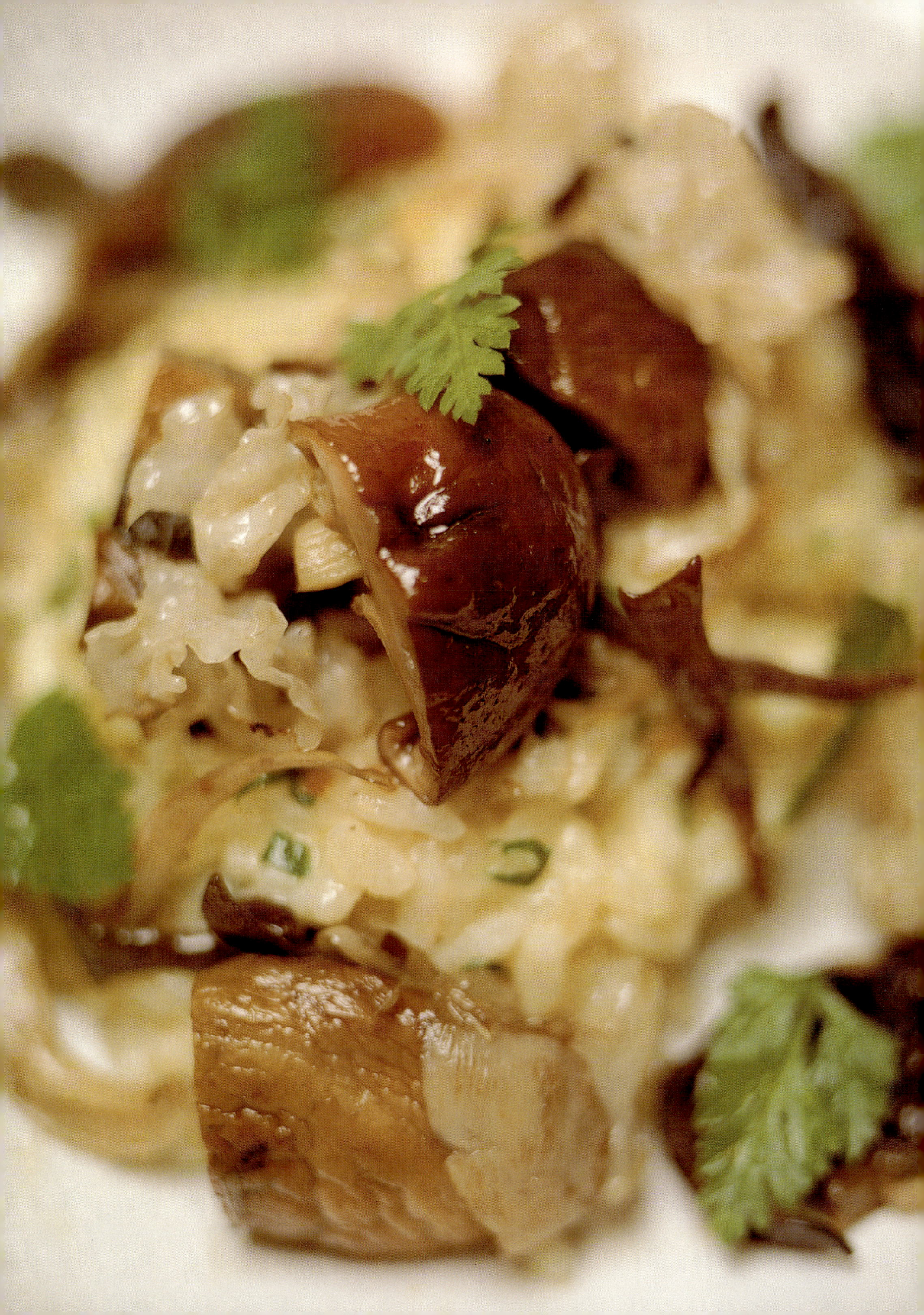

MORETON BAY BUGS ON LINGUINE WITH HERB OIL

INGREDIENTS

600 gm Moreton Bay Bug Tails (shelled and de-veined)

100 ml Aioli (see recipe page 153)

100 ml Herb Oil (see recipe page 153)

50 ml Olive Oil

PASTA DOUGH

300 gm Plain Flour (sifted)

3 Eggs

2 Egg Yolks

1 desp Olive Oil

1 pinch Salt

2 teasp Squid Ink

METHOD

- Combine flour and eggs in a food processor, add oil, salt and squid ink.
- Remove and knead to a smooth dough on bench, wrap in cling wrap and refrigerate.
- When chilled, divide dough into three and flour lightly.
- Pass dough through linguine cutter after obtaining desired thickness on pasta roller.
- Flour lightly and rest (well separated over wooden spoons) for 10 mins.
- Bring 3 litres salted water and 50 ml olive oil to the boil in a large pot.
- Cook pasta until 'al dente' (2 mins), drain in colander.
- Heat olive oil in a teflon pan and cook bugs for 5 mins on medium heat.
- Roll pasta on a carving fork to give 'bun' shape and place in the centre of each bowl.
- Rest bugs on top of pasta and drizzle with aioli.
- Spoon herb oil around outside of pasta and serve.

NOTE Dried squid ink pasta is available from good delicatessans.

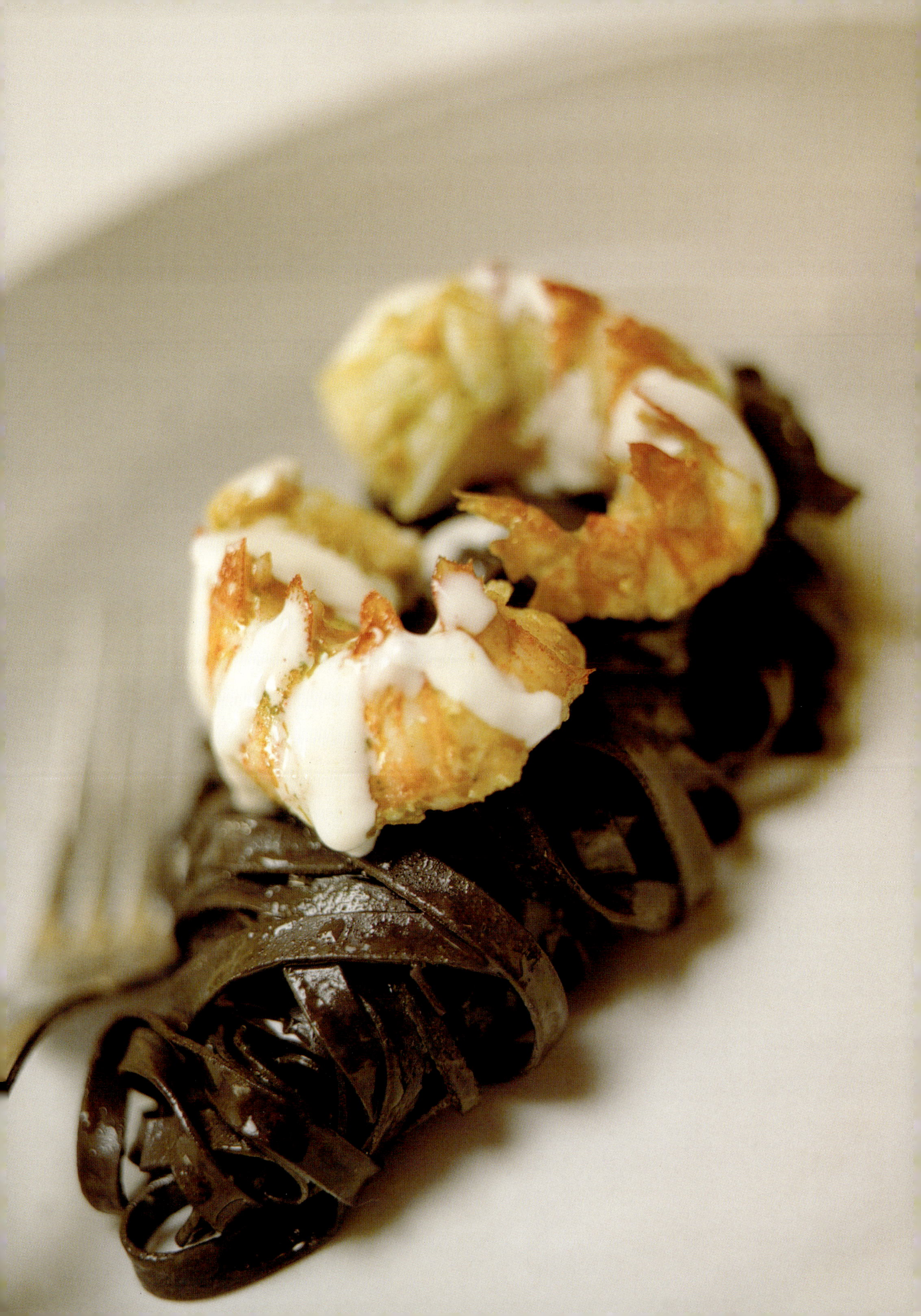

CALAMARI TOSSED WITH SPAGHETTINI & TAPENADE

INGREDIENTS 400 gm Calamari
(cleaned and cut into fat rings)

350 gm dried Spaghettini Pasta

TAPENADE

200 gm Kalamata Olives (pitted)

30 gm Anchovies

30 gm Capers

4 cloves Garlic (peeled)

75 ml Extra Virgin Olive Oil

1 Lemon (juice only)

1/2 cup Italian Parsley Leaves

6 Sweet Basil Leaves

METHOD
- Combine all ingredients for tapenade in food processor and blend on high speed to a smooth paste.
- Cook pasta until 'al dente' in a large pot of salted water with a little olive oil.
- Drain pasta and put into a large bowl. Pour tapenade over pasta.
- Heat 50 ml vegetable oil until very hot in a large pan or wok.
- Cook calamari for 30 secs and mix into pasta and sauce.
- Divide into six bowls and serve.

CHERMOULAH CRUSTED SALMON

INGREDIENTS

6 x 150 gm Atlantic Salmon Fillets (bones and skin removed)

12 Southern Gold Potatoes (washed)

12 Lemon Wedges

200 ml Herb Oil (see recipe page 153)

MARINADE

6 tblsp Extra Virgin Olive Oil

1 Salad Onion (peeled and finely chopped)

2 cloves Garlic (crushed)

1 pinch Saffron Strands

4 tblsp Parsley (chopped)

4 tblsp Coriander Leaves (chopped)

1 teasp Black Pepper (ground)

1 teasp Cumin (ground)

2 teasp Turmeric

2 teasp Ginger (grated)

1 teasp Paprika

1 teasp Salt

2 Lemons (juice and zest only)

METHOD

- Combine all ingredients for marinade in food processor on high speed.
- Pour over salmon fillets, cover and refrigerate for minimum 2 hrs.
- Steam or poach potatoes in salted water.
- Remove salmon from marinade.
- Heat vegetable oil in a teflon pan until very hot, cook salmon for 3 mins. each side.
- Arrange salmon, potatoes and lemon wedges on plates, drizzle with herb oil and serve.

GNOCCHI & PRAWNS IN TOMATO SAUCE

INGREDIENTS

24 large Tiger Prawns
(shelled and de-veined)

25 ml Vegetable Oil

GNOCCHI

250 gm Potatoes
(Kipfler, Bintje or other waxy style)

25 gm Butter

2 Egg Yolks

1/3 cup Plain Flour

2 pinches Nutmeg

80 gm Parmesan (grated)

2 desp Semolina

TOMATO SAUCE

500 gm Roma Tomatoes
(blanched, peeled and diced)

or

1 small tin Italian Peeled Tomatoes (diced)

1/2 large Brown Onion
(finely chopped)

4 cloves Garlic
(peeled and crushed)

50 ml Extra Virgin Olive Oil

18 large fresh Basil Leaves

METHOD

- Peel and boil potatoes until soft, drain well and mash finely.
- Add butter, egg yolks, flour, nutmeg, parmesan, and semolina. Season with salt and pepper and mix well.
- Bring 4 litres of lightly salted water to the boil in a heavy pot. With a teaspoon, drop small amounts of mixture into water (use small amounts at a time to avoid sticking).
- After gnocchi is cooked (3 to 5 mins), remove from pot with a slotted spoon and drop into cold water.
- Warm olive oil in a heavy based pot, add chopped onion and cook until transparent, add garlic and tomato, simmer for 20 mins.
- Saute prawns in vegetable oil until almost cooked, add tomato sauce, gnocchi and basil (retain 1/3 basil leaves and slice finely for garnish).
- Simmer for 3 to 4 mins, divide evenly into six bowls, garnish and serve immediately.

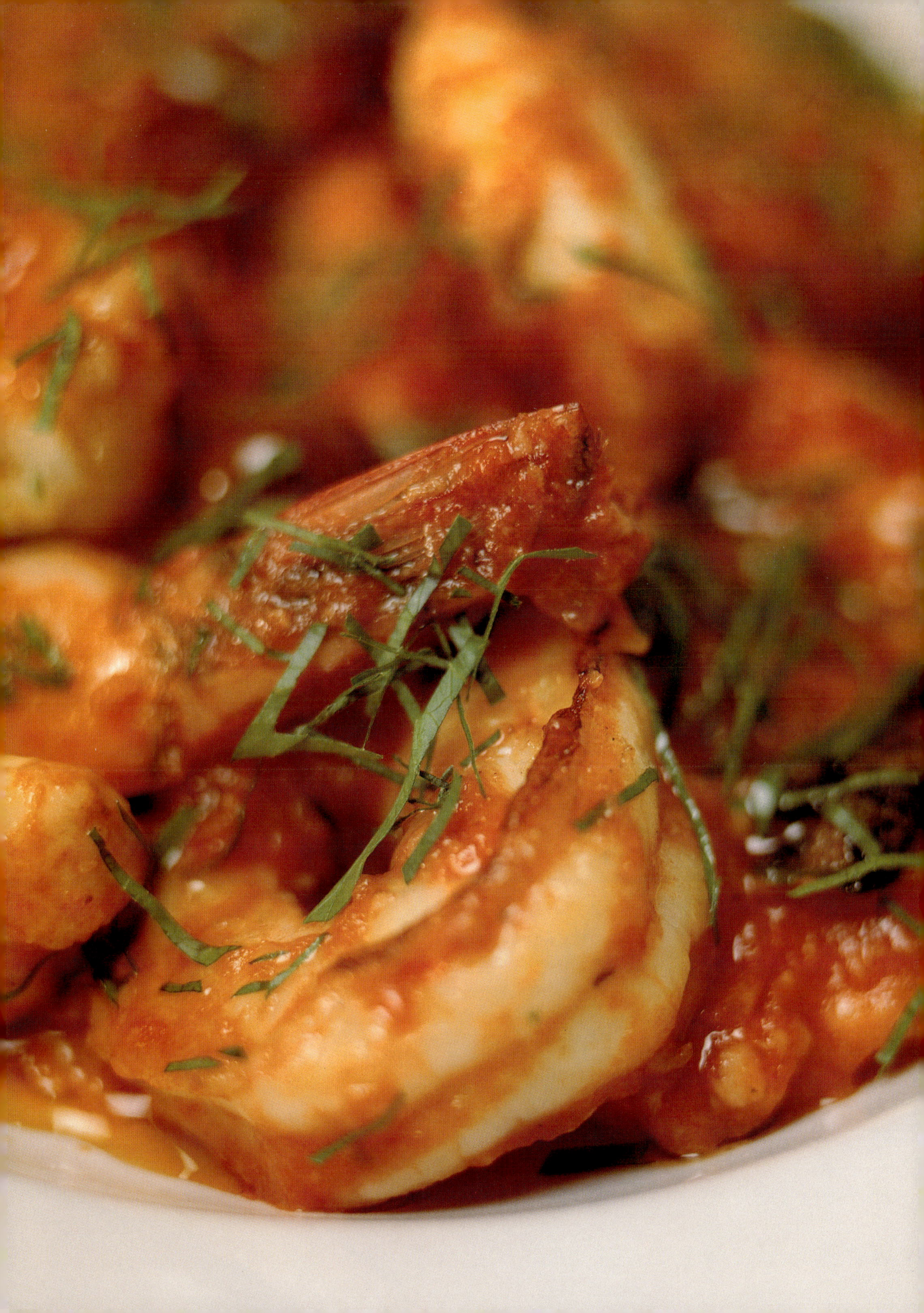

SEARED CALVE'S LIVER ON BRAISED RADICCHIO

INGREDIENTS

900 gm Calve's Liver

1 1/2 small Radicchio

6 desp Onion Confit
(see recipe page 158)

1 cup Demi Glace
(see recipe page 149)

75 ml Balsamic Vinegar

1 desp Olive Oil

METHOD

- Remove all sinew and membrane from calve's liver and slice thinly (4 mm).
- Remove outside leaves from radicchio and cut into quarters vertically (keeping stem intact at the base of each piece).
- Heat olive oil in a braising pan on low heat.
- Cook radicchio until slightly wilted.
- Add vinegar, cover and cook for 5 mins.
- Add water, demi glace and return to heat for further 10 mins.
- Remove radicchio from pan and strain sauce.
- Warm onion confit gently in a small pot.
- Cook liver in a very hot teflon pan for 30 secs to 1 min until liver is evenly sealed but still rare in the centre.
- Spoon onion into the centre of six plates, rest radicchio on onion and drape liver over.
- Spoon sauce around plate and serve.

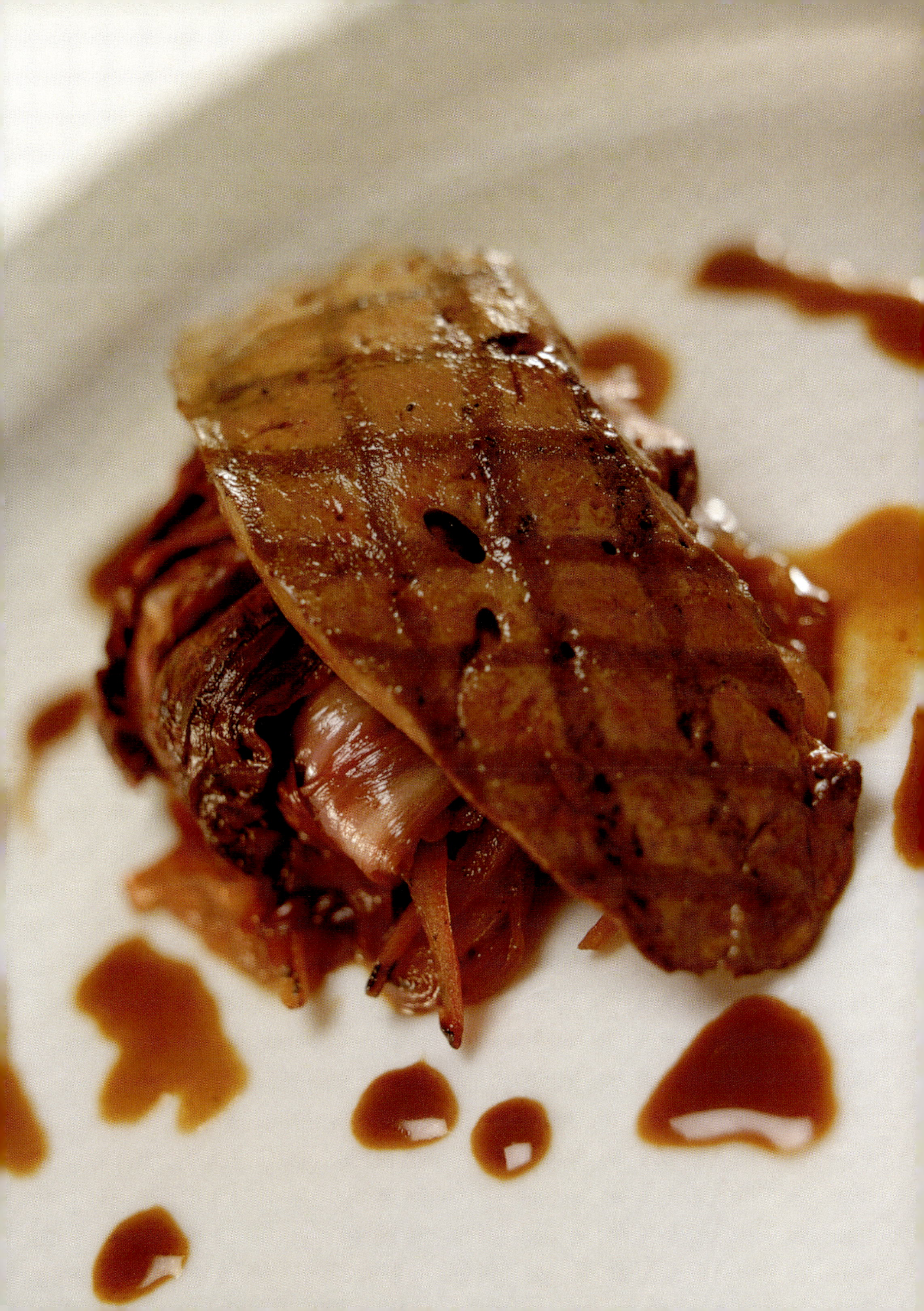

LAMB WITH NICOISE VEGETABLES

INGREDIENTS

6 x 180 gm Lamb Loins

3 small Salad Onions (peeled)

1 Japanese Eggplant

1 small Green Zucchini

1 small Yellow Zucchini

1 small Fennel Bulb

1/2 Red Capsicum

1/4 Yellow Capsicum

12 cloves Roasted Garlic
(see recipe page 159)

200 ml Aioli
(see recipe page 153)

100 ml Olive Oil

200 ml Lamb Jus
(see recipe page 150)

METHOD

- Cut onions into eighths with core intact.
- Cut eggplant and zucchini into 1/2 cm rounds.
- Trim and cut fennel and capsicums into bite size pieces.
- Toss vegetables in olive oil and sear on grill or in a heavy pan until cooked lightly then set aside.
- Sear lamb loins on grill or in a heavy pan for 2 mins each side.
- Add lamb to roasted garlic and vegetables then place in a hot oven until vegetables are hot.
- Divide vegetables between six plates, carve lamb lengthways and drape over vegetables.
- Drizzle aioli lightly around plate and serve.

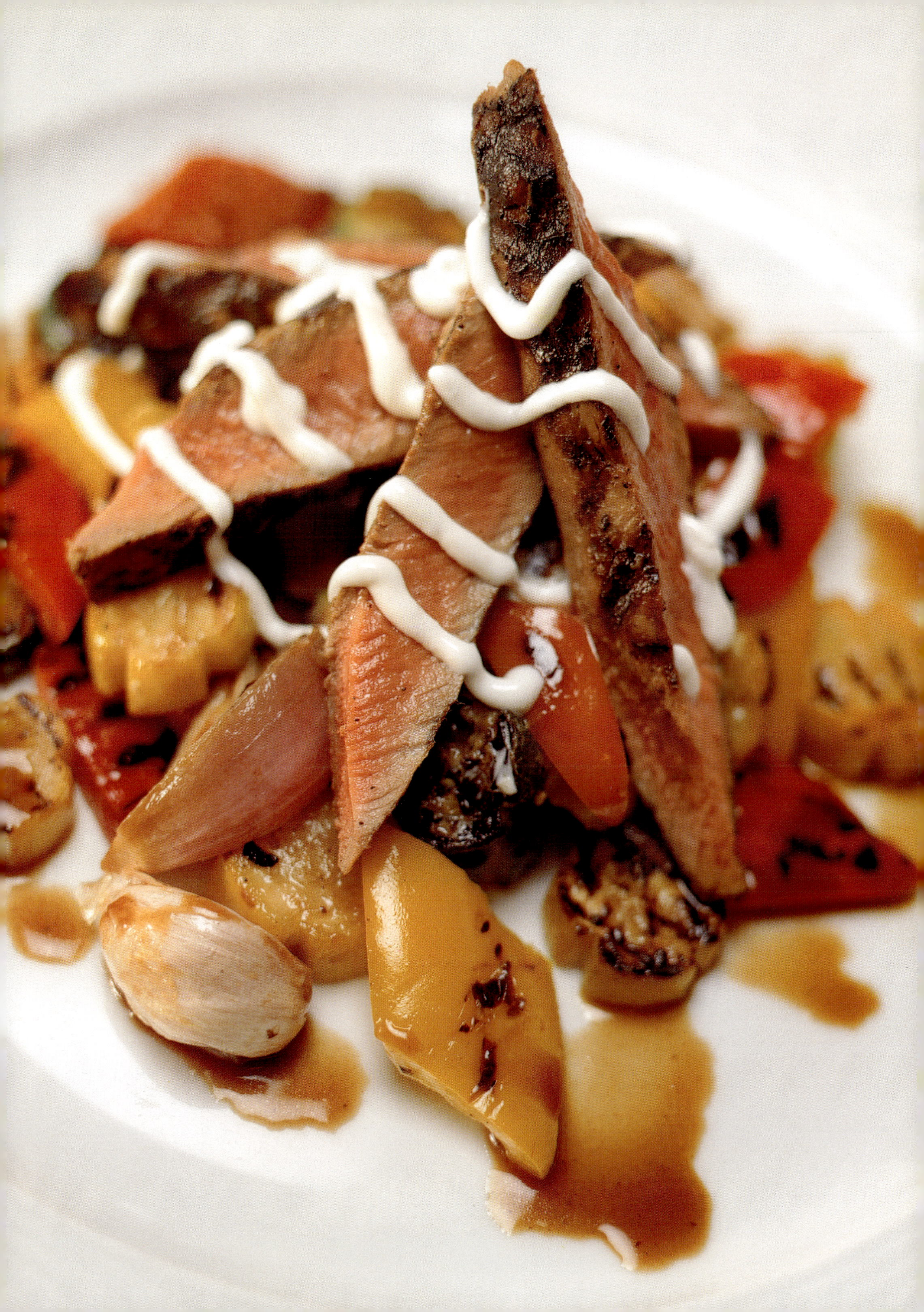

CHICKEN BREAST WITH BORLOTTI BEANS & TUSCAN SAUSAGE

INGREDIENTS

6 Chicken Breasts
(size 12 with skin on)

2 Smoked Tuscan Sausages
(skin removed and cut into strips)

24 cloves Roast Garlic
(see recipe page 159)

24 Button Mushrooms

12 Shallots (sliced)

100 gm Borlotti Beans (dried)

300 ml Chicken Jus
(see recipe page 151)

Italian Parsley

METHOD

- Soak borlotti beans in 500 ml cold water overnight.
- Bring borlotti beans to the boil in 1 litre water, reduce to simmer for 45 mins and strain.
- Pre-heat oven and tray to 200°C.
- Trim excess fat from chicken breasts and seal, skin side down, in a little vegetable oil in a hot pan.
- Remove breasts to oven tray and cook for 12 mins in oven.
- Trim button mushrooms and cut in half, saute on high heat until lightly coloured. Add shallots and cook for 1 min.
- Add garlic, sausage, borlotti beans and chicken jus, warm gently.
- Divide bean mix between six plates and garnish with sprigs of Italian parsley. Rest chicken breasts over beans and serve.

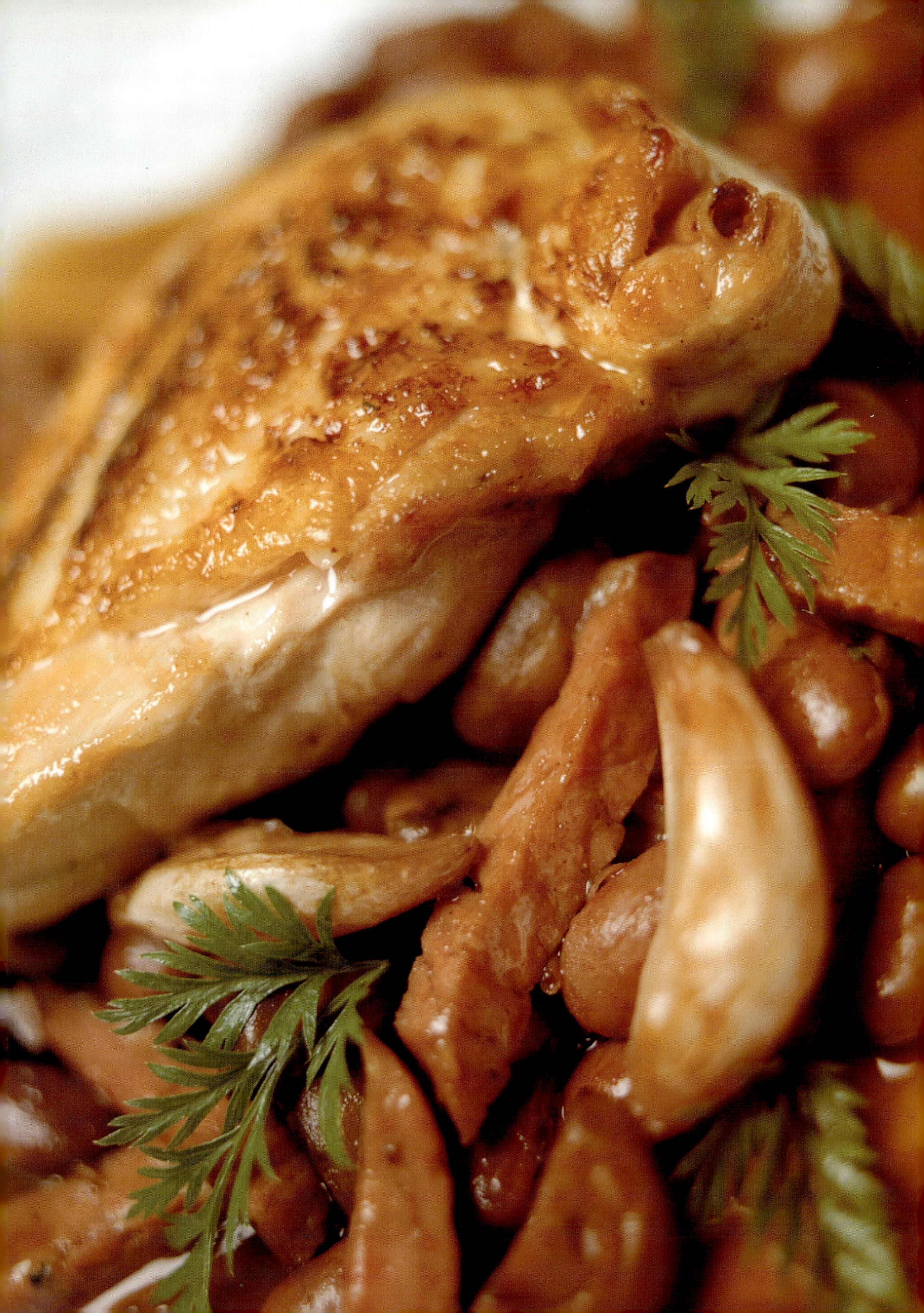

BRAISED VEAL SHANKS WITH SOFT POLENTA

INGREDIENTS 6 small Veal Shanks

BRAISAGE (sauce)

1 medium Carrot
(peeled and chopped)

1 stick Celery (chopped)

1 medium Brown Onion
(peeled and chopped)

1 whole Garlic
(split horizontally and chopped)

400 ml Tomatoes (crushed)

2 sprigs Thyme

2 Bay Leaves

12 Black Peppercorns

400 ml Demi Glace
(see recipe page 149)

GARNISH

3 small Salad Onions
(cut vertically into sixths)

2 medium Carrots
(peeled and cut into sixths)

1 Swede
(peeled and cut into twelfths)

1 medium Parsnip
(peeled and cut into sixths)

18 cloves Roast Garlic
(see recipe page 159)

Chervil

Polenta (see recipe page 157)

METHOD
- Pre-heat oven and heavy oven dish to 180°C. Trim excess skin and sinew from shanks then lay in dish with 50 ml vegetable oil and roast for 15 mins.
- Add chopped vegetables and cook for further 15 mins.
- Heat tomatoes, thyme, bay leaves, peppercorns and demi glace in a medium pot. Pour sauce into oven dish, cover with foil and return to oven for 1 hr.
- Remove shanks from dish and pass liquid through a fine sieve.
- Return shanks, liquid and garnish vegetables to oven for a further 30 mins.
- Spoon polenta into six bowls, stand one veal shank in centre of each bowl.
- Spoon braisage and vegetables around polenta, garnish with chervil and serve.

NOTE Shanks will have a better flavour if cooked the day before and re-heated to serve. If small shanks are not available, get your butcher to cut shanks into smaller (Osso Bucco) pieces.

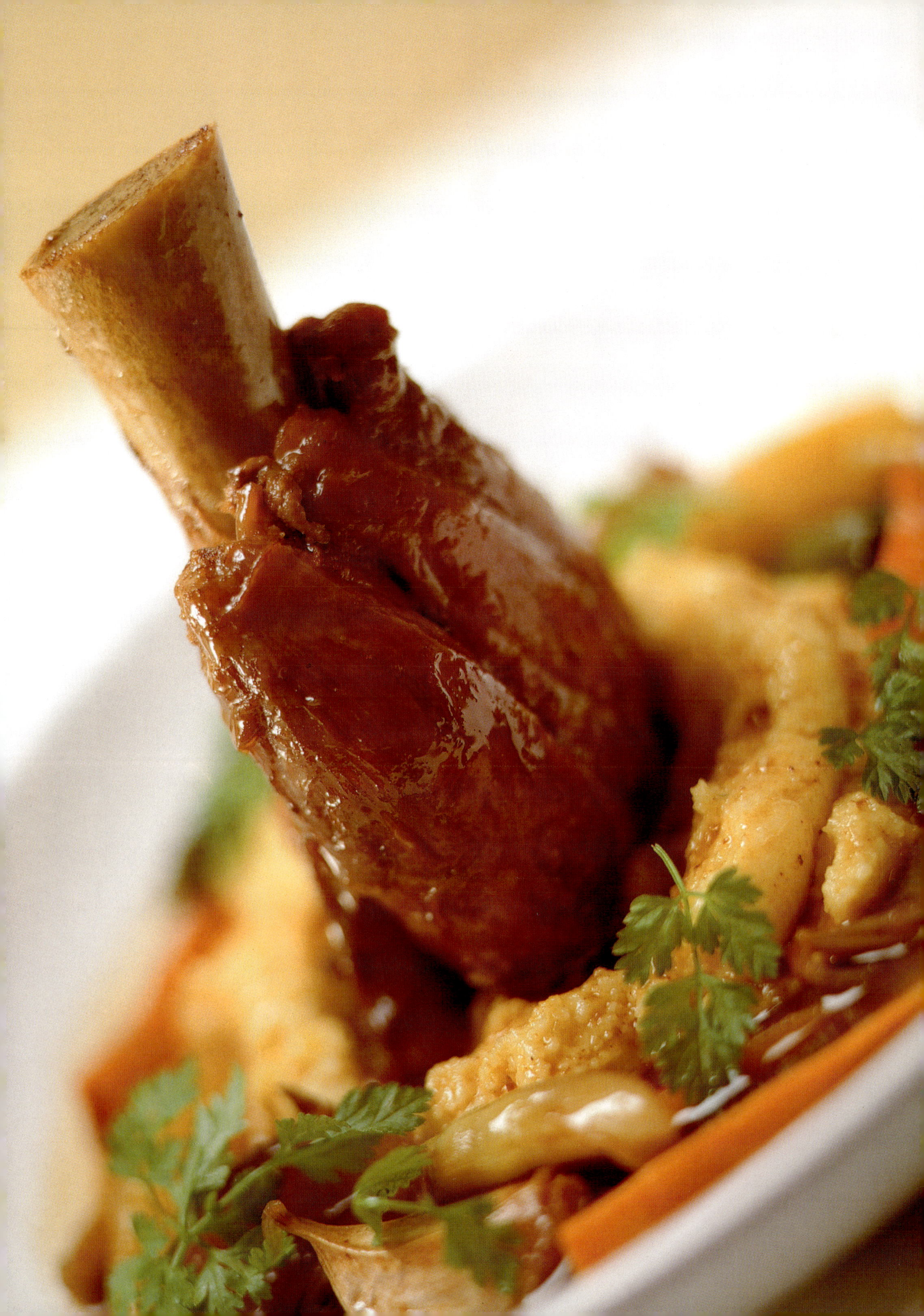

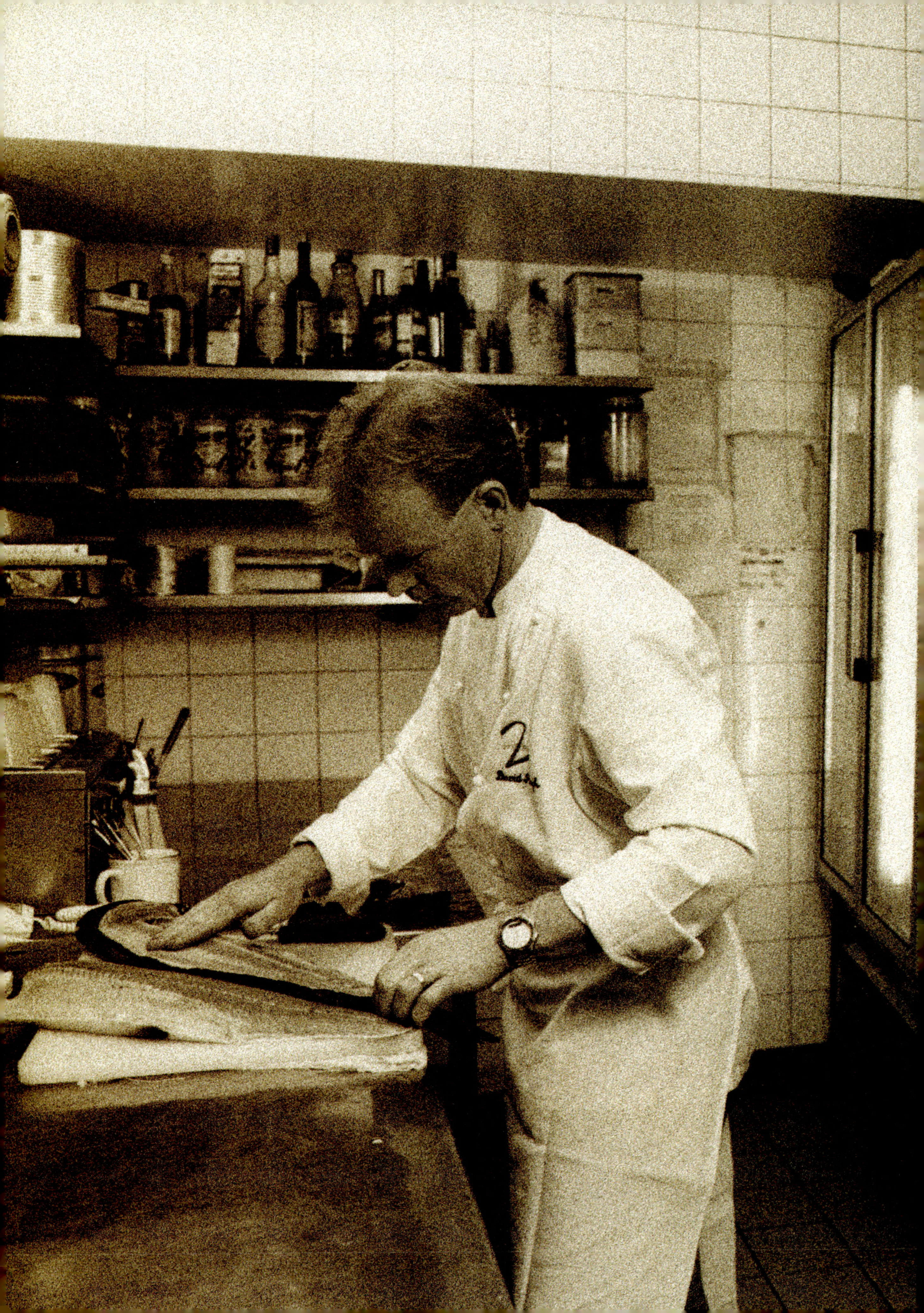

MODERN CLASSICS

A collection of legendary dishes, some of our personal favourites.

FRESHLY SHUCKED OYSTERS WITH RED WINE VINEGAR DIPPING SAUCE

INGREDIENTS 36 large un-opened Oysters

DIPPING SAUCE

150 ml Red Wine Vinegar

3 Shallots
(peeled and finely chopped)

Black Pepper (cracked)

Ice (cracked)

Seaweed (optional)

METHOD
- Mix red wine vinegar and shallots, season to taste with black pepper.
- Just prior to serving, open oyster with a sharp, double-sided oyster knife.
- Cut top muscle securing lid and remove any grit. Retain as much liquid in shell as possible. Do not rinse in fresh water.
- Mound cracked ice in the base of six bowls and cover with seaweed.
- Arrange oysters over cracked ice, pour dipping sauce in separate dishes and serve.

NOTE Always hold oyster in a heavy cloth while opening. Oysters will have much better flavour when served immediately after opening. Un-opened oysters can be ordered from most good seafood outlets.

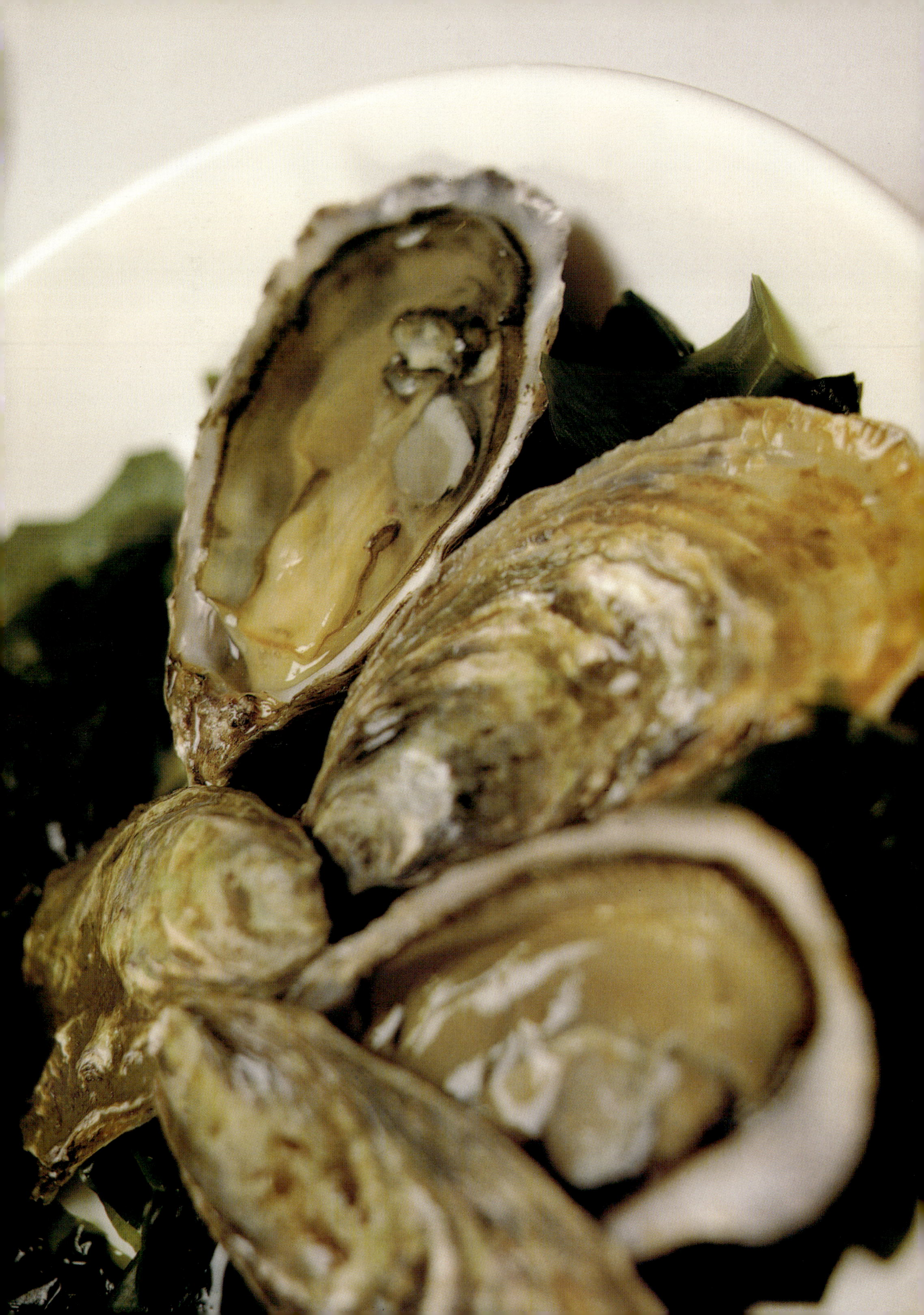

ROAST GARLIC & BROWN ONION SOUP

INGREDIENTS
1200 ml Chicken Stock
(see recipe page 148)

500 gm Brown Onions
(peeled and thinly sliced)

20 cloves Roast Garlic
(see recipe page 159)

50 ml Vegetable Oil

50 ml Madeira

METHOD
- Saute sliced onions in vegetable oil in a large heavy based pot until golden brown.
- Add Madeira and reduce by half, add stock, bring to the boil and reduce to simmer for 20 mins.
- Remove skin from roast garlic and blend with a little stock in a food processor. Add puree to soup and simmer for 5 mins.
- Warm six soup bowls in oven, divide soup evenly and serve.

NOTE
Soup should be served with crusty bread or bruschetta.

WILD & FIELD MUSHROOM BROTH

INGREDIENTS

500 gm Field Mushrooms (chopped)

500 gm Shitake Mushrooms (chopped)

1 small Brown Onion (chopped)

1 Leek (chopped)

4 cloves Garlic (peeled and crushed)

1 litre Chicken Stock (see recipe page 148)

50 gm Butter

1 despn Chives (chopped)

1 despn Italian Parsely (chopped)

METHOD

- Melt butter in a large heavy based pot, add mushrooms, onion, leek and garlic.
- Cook on high heat for approx. 4 mins. Add chicken stock and return to boil.
- Reduce heat and simmer for 20 mins. Remove from heat and blend, a little at a time, in a food processor or vitamiser until smooth.
- Divide into six bowls and serve topped with chopped herbs.

NOTE

Sour dough or Panini bread toasted with olive oil and crushed garlic makes a great accompaniment to this dish. A few drops of truffle or porcini oil will greatly enhance this dish.

ROCKET & COS SALAD WITH ANCHOVY MAYONNAISE

INGREDIENTS

ANCHOVY MAYONNAISE

2 Egg Yolks

2 cloves Garlic

2 tblsp Dijon Mustard

1 1/2 tblsp Capers

10 Anchovy Fillets

1 teasp Tabasco

2 tblsp Red Wine Vinegar

Black Pepper (fresh ground)

500 ml Olive Oil

SALAD

2 Cos Lettuce (cleaned and washed)

100 gm Rocket (washed)

12 Anchovy Fillets

12 slices Prosciutto

1/3 Baguette

100 gm Parmesan (shaved)

Black Pepper (cracked)

METHOD

- Blend all mayonnaise ingredients, except oil, in a food processor until smooth.
- Add olive oil slowly until desired texture is reached, add pepper to taste.
- Lay prosciutto flat on a baking sheet and cook in 160°C oven until crisp (approx. 10 mins).
- Slice baguette thinly, lay flat on baking sheet and cook in 160°C oven until lightly coloured and crisp (7 mins).
- Toss cos and rocket in a large bowl and divide half the cos and rocket between six bowls.
- Layer half of prosciutto, anchovy, baguette and parmesan over cos and rocket leaves and drizzle lightly with mayonnaise.
- Repeat layering sequence, drizzle with remaining mayonnaise, garnish with black pepper to taste and serve.

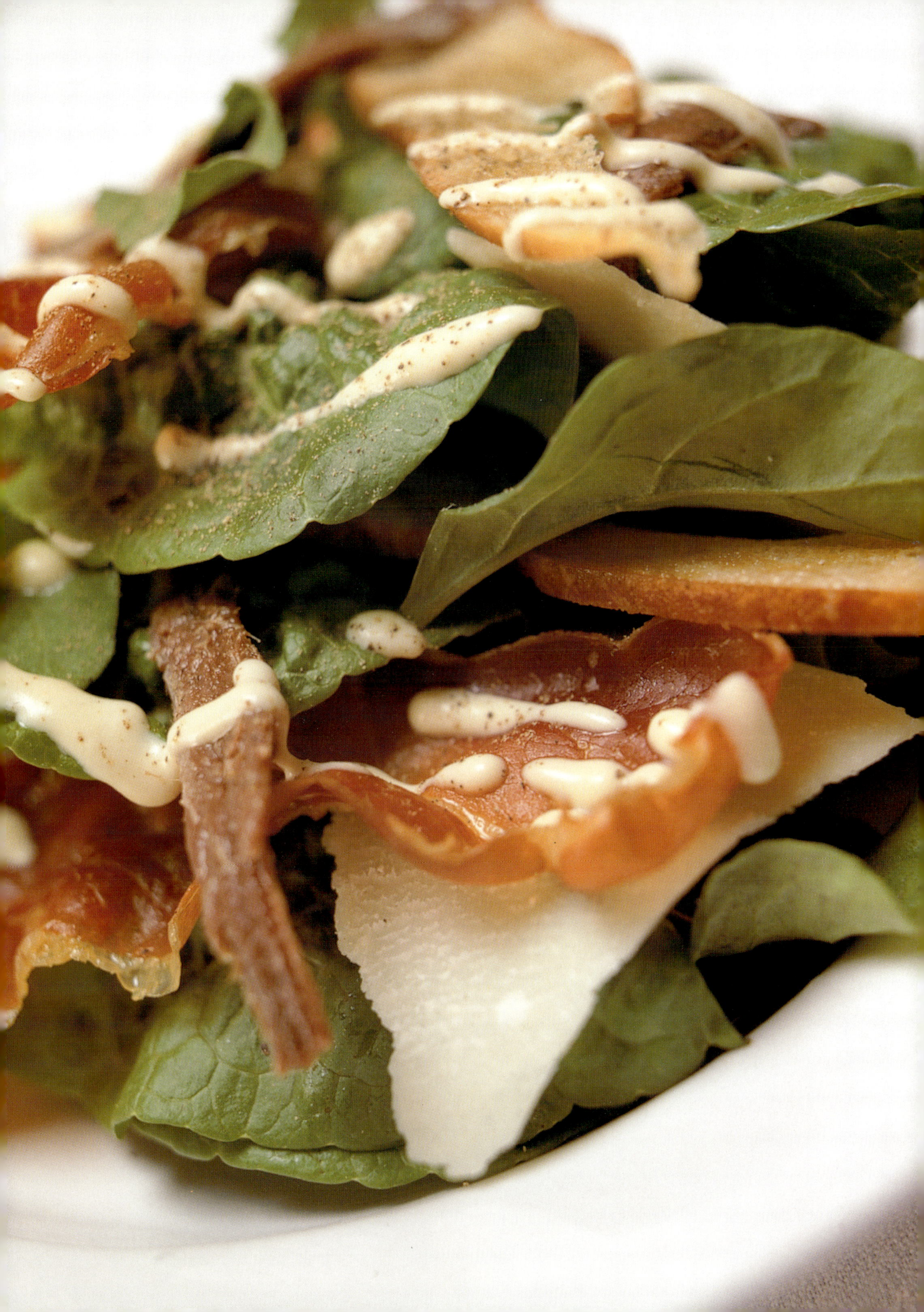

FRESHWATER YABBIES WITH TRUFFLE & WALNUT OIL DRESSING

INGREDIENTS

24 Freshwater Yabbies (approx 90 gm each)

2 litres Court Bouillon (see recipe page 149)

120 gm Mesclun Salad Mix (washed and dried)

12 Green Beans

12 Asparagus Spears (peeled)

12 Walnut Kernels

DRESSING

150 ml Extra Virgin Olive Oil

50 ml Walnut Oil

50 ml Black Truffle Oil

2 tblsp Sherry Vinegar

1 teasp Dijon Mustard

1 teasp Lemon Juice

METHOD

- Bring court bouillon to the boil in a large pot, immerse yabbies in bouillon and return to boil.
- Remove yabbies from pot and allow to cool.
- Remove shell and veins from yabbies, slice lengthways and refrigerate.
- Bring 1 litre water to the boil, blanch asparagus and beans for 1 min.
- Remove from heat and refresh under cold running water.
- Cut beans and asparagus into thirds on angle.
- Whisk oils, vinegar, mustard and lemon juice together, season to taste with salt and pepper.
- Warm walnuts in a teflon pan on low heat for 2 mins.
- Arrange mesclun leaves in centre of six plates, scatter asparagus, beans and walnuts around salad leaves.
- Arrange yabbies around outside of plate, dress liberally and serve.

OMELETTE OF WILD MUSHROOM & BLACK TRUFFLE

(SERVES 4)

INGREDIENTS

OMELETTE

75 gm Shitake Mushrooms (cut into quarters)

75 gm Oyster Mushrooms (cut into strips)

100 gm Pine Mushrooms (sliced)

2 desp Black Truffle (finely chopped)

2 Shallots (sliced)

4 tblsp Olive Oil

100 ml Vegetable Oil

12 large Eggs (whisked)

1 pinch Salt

GARNISH

Chervil

12 fine slices Black Truffle

30 ml Black Truffle Oil

METHOD

- Heat olive oil in a heavy based pan on high heat and saute mushrooms one variety at a time.
- Saute shallots and combine with mushrooms.
- Heat omelette pan to medium heat, add 25 ml vegetable oil and pour in a quarter of egg mix (omelettes can only be made one at a time).
- Stir with fork and keep mix soft, place 1/4 of mushroom mix in center, season to taste with salt and pepper, fold omelette over and tap down onto plate.
- Garnish with chervil, truffle slices and a light drizzle of truffle oil.
- Serve immediately.

NOTE

Some practice at making omelettes is advised before making this dish. Do not attempt this dish for larger groups as each omelette takes at least 2 mins to make. A partially broken omelette can be re-shaped by moulding between hands on the plate. Unavailable mushrooms can be substituted with dried forest mushrooms soaked in water overnight.

SCRAMBLED EGGS & SMOKED SALMON WITH CAVIAR

INGREDIENTS
12 large Eggs
200 gm Unsalted Butter
100 ml Cream
12 sheets Smoked Salmon
30 gm Sevruga Caviar
30 gm Salmon Roe
6 slices Sour Dough Bread (toasted)

METHOD
- Whisk eggs and season lightly.
- Add cream and half butter to a heavy pan on low heat.
- Add eggs stirring continuously until mix thickens.
- Whisk in remaining butter.
- Place toasted sour dough on warm plates.
- Lay smoked salmon over toast.
- Spoon scrambled eggs over salmon and garnish with caviar and salmon roe. Serve immediately.

NOTE As well as an easy entree this dish can make a decadent breakfast or brunch.

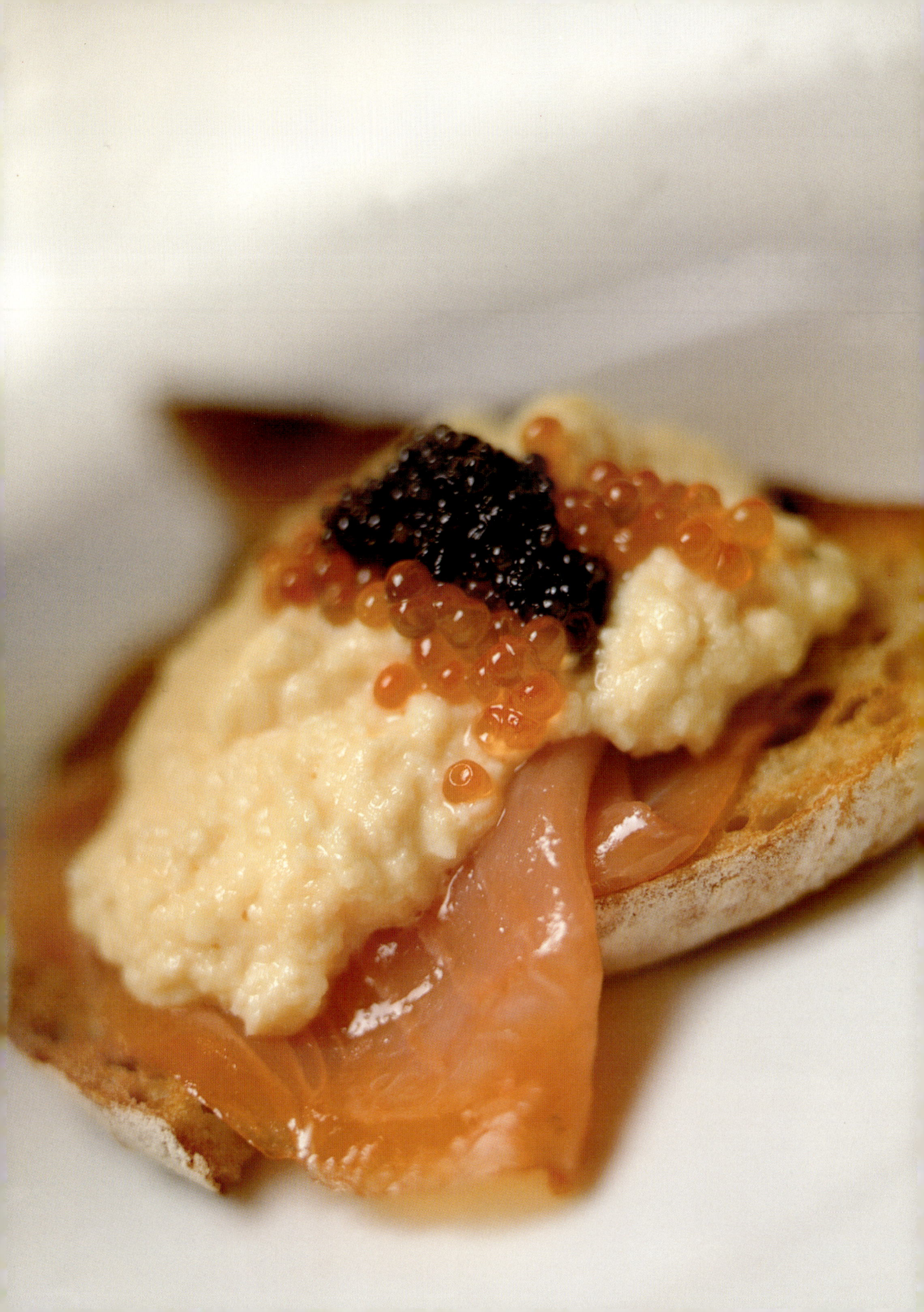

TARTLET OF LAMB'S BRAINS ON ONION CONFIT

INGREDIENTS

9 whole Lamb's Brains

2 litres Court Bouillon
(see recipe page 149)

60 gm English Spinach

50 ml Vegetable Oil

6 cloves Roast Garlic
(see recipe page 159)

150 ml Lamb Jus
(see recipe page 150)

Onion Confit
(see recipe page 158)

TARTLET SHELLS

250 gm Plain Flour

200 gm Unsalted Butter (chilled)

1 large Egg

1 Egg Yolk

Pinch Salt

METHOD

- Combine all ingredients for pastry in a food processor until lightly bound.
- Rest pastry for 20 mins then roll on a floured bench until 3 mm thick. Roll into tartlet shells and press into corners.
- Bake blind in a 180°C oven for 25 mins.
- Bring court bouillon to the boil in a large pot, add brains and remove pot from heat immediately. Allow brains to cool in bouillon, then remove and trim into lobes removing any excess membrane and skin.
- Divide onion confit into six tartlet shells, rest garlic beside confit, warm in a 150°C oven for 5 mins.
- Saute English spinach in a hot, heavy based pan in 25 ml vegetable oil until wilted (20 secs).
- Saute lambs brains in a heavy based pan in 25 ml vegetable oil until well coloured both sides.
- Remove tartlet shells from oven tray and place in center of plates. Rest English spinach in tartlet shells.
- Arrange brains in tartlet shells, place garlic over brains, drizzle with warm lamb jus and serve.

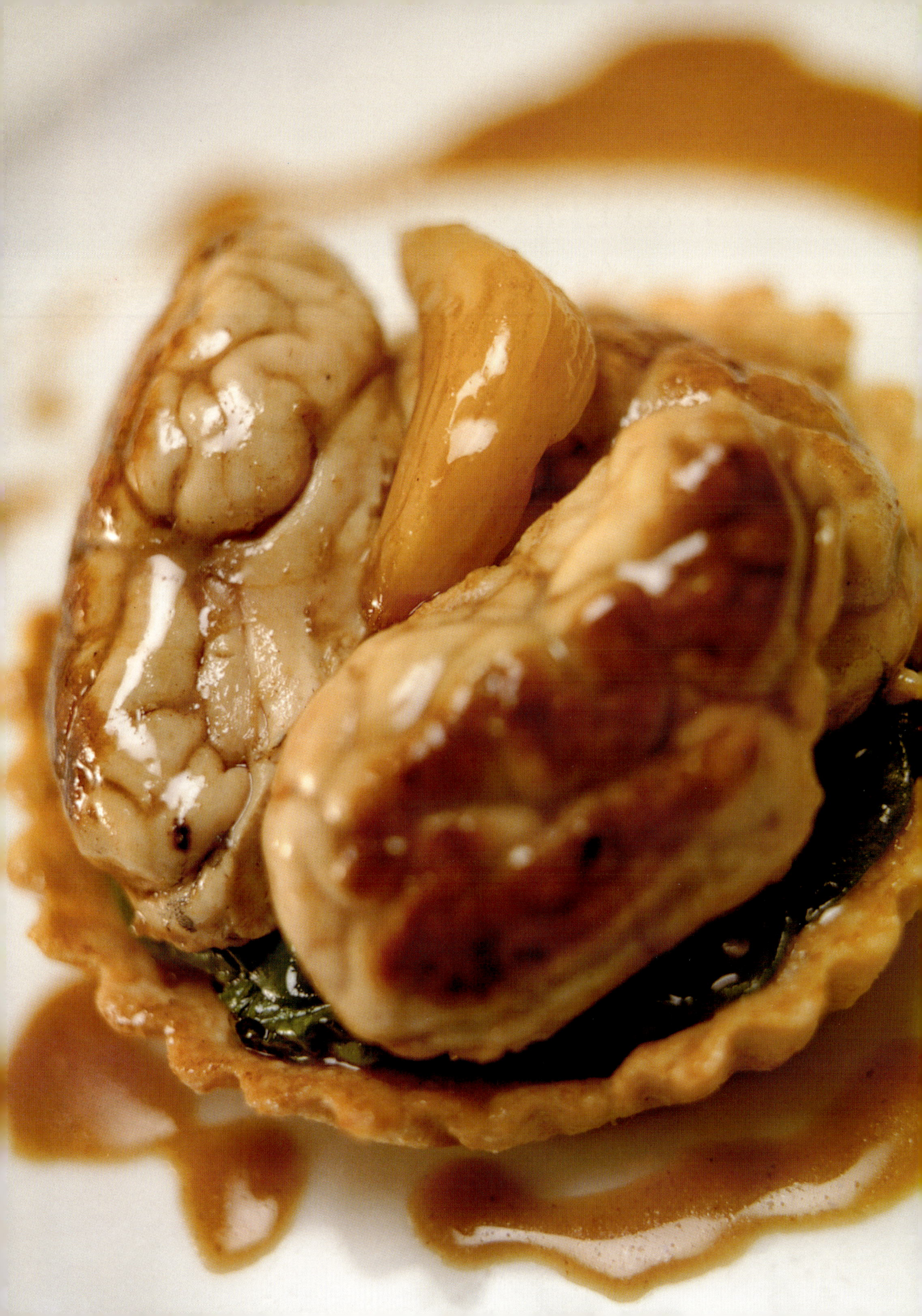

SEARED VEAL KIDNEYS WITH BACON & SEEDED MUSTARD

INGREDIENTS

400 gm Veal Kidneys
(fat and sinew removed)

250 ml Milk

180 gm Bacon (thick slices)

18 Button Mushrooms

18 Roast Shallots
(see recipe page 159)

6 slices Sour Dough Bread
(toasted)

300 ml Mustard Sauce
(see recipe page 151)

Chervil

METHOD

- Dice veal kidneys and soak in milk for 2 hrs. Remove from milk, drain and pat dry with paper towelling.
- Cut bacon into large batons and saute in a hot pan until crisp outside.
- Saute mushrooms in a hot pan until lightly coloured.
- Saute kidneys in a hot pan until lightly sealed. Add mushrooms, bacon and shallots, cook until all ingredients are hot.
- Place sour dough toast in centre of plates and spoon kidneys over toast.
- Coat liberally with mustard sauce, garnish with chervil and serve.

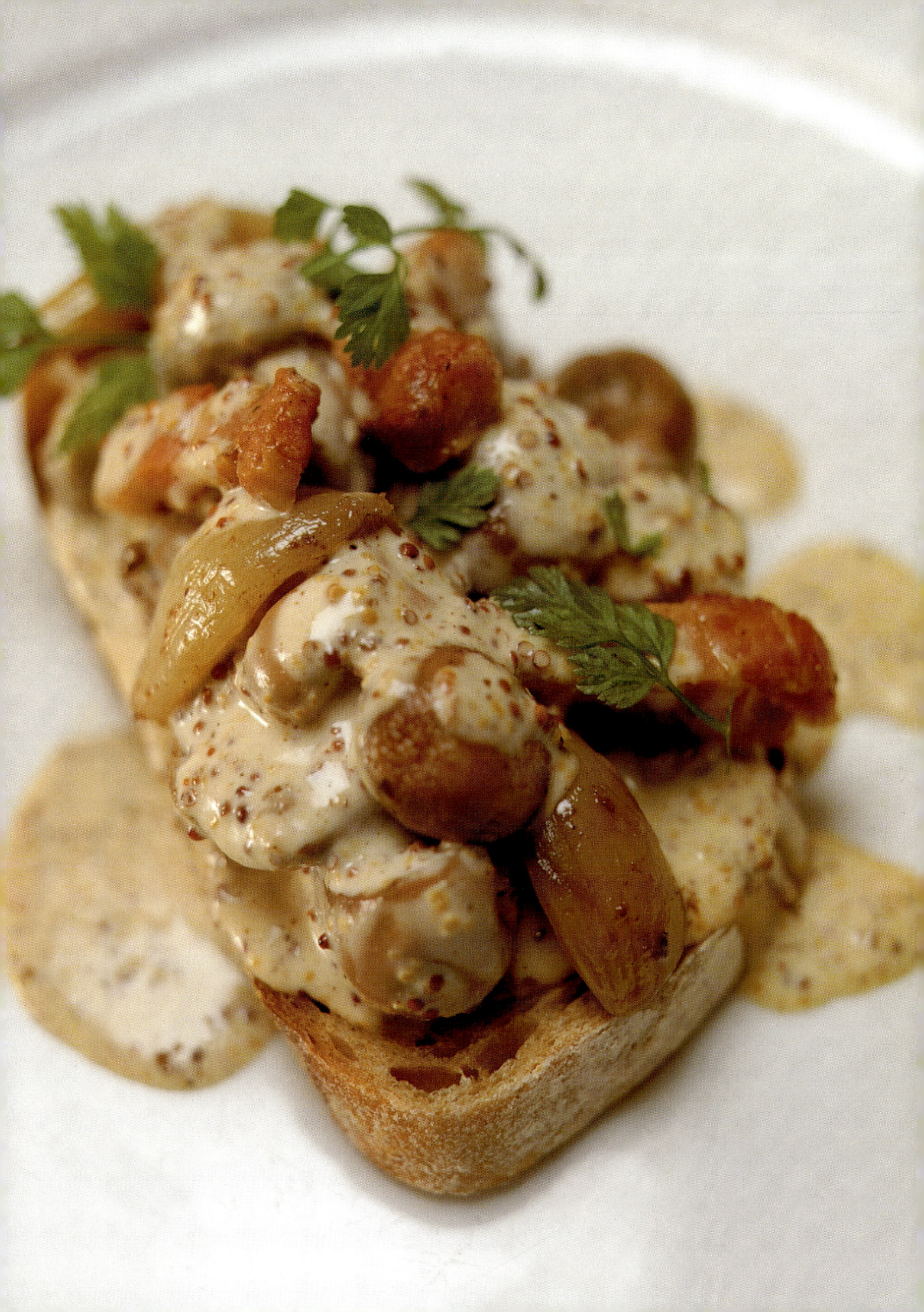

FILLETS OF REEF FISH WITH SAFFRON BEURRE BLANC

INGREDIENTS

6 x 150 gm Reef Fish Fillets
30 ml Vegetable Oil
50 gm Butter (soft)

SAUCE

2 pinches Saffron Strands
40 gm Shallots (sliced)
750 ml White Wine Vinegar
6 Black Peppercorns

750 ml White Wine (reisling or other unwooded wine)
250 gm Unsalted Butter (soft)

GARNISH

80 gm English Spinach
20 gm Butter
12 New Potatoes

METHOD

- Bring all ingredients for sauce except butter to the boil in a heavy pot, reduce by 7/8 (approx. 190 ml).
- Strain into a stainless steel bowl and slowly whisk in butter.
- Bring new potatoes and 1.5 litres salted water to the boil and cook until fork can be removed cleanly (approx. 5 to 7 mins)
- Ensure all skin and bones are removed from fish.
- Pre-heat oven and baking tray to 200°C.
- Heat vegetable oil in a teflon pan on medium heat, seal fillets well on each side.
- Place fillets on a pre-heated, buttered, oven tray, cook in oven for 6 mins.
- Toss spinach and butter in a pre-heated pan until wilted (30 secs), divide spinach evenly between six plates.
- Rest fillets over spinach and spoon sauce around outside of fillets.
- Place new potatoes beside fillets and serve.

NOTE

Richer flavoured fish such as red emperor, snapper or pearl perch are better suited to this dish as the saffron may overpower the lighter flavours of fish such as coral trout or maori wrasse. Cooking times for this dish may vary depending on the thickness of the fillets.

ROAST GUINEA FOWL ON CREAMED CABBAGE

INGREDIENTS

3 Guinea Fowl (size 10)

30 ml Vegetable Oil

350 ml Chicken Jus
(see recipe page 151)

4 dried Juniper Berries
(crushed)

GARNISH

1/4 Savoy Cabbage
(or 1/2 Sugar Loaf Cabbage)

2 Bacon Rashers
(thick sliced and cut into batons)

1 small Carrot
(peeled and small diced)

1/2 Brown Onion
(peeled and small diced)

1 small Leek (outside leaves removed and thinly sliced)

1/2 Celery Stick
(peeled and small diced)

200 ml Cream

30 ml Vegetable Oil

METHOD

- Bring juniper berries and chicken jus to the boil. Reduce heat, simmer for 10 mins and strain.
- Brush Guinea fowls and oven tray with vegetable oil. Cook Guinea fowls with one breast side down in a pre-heated oven at 200°C for 10 mins.
- Turn birds on to other breast and cook for further 8 mins.
- Remove birds from oven, carve off legs and return to tray skin side up. Replace birds on their backs and cook for further 5 mins in baking tray.
- Remove birds and legs from oven and rest in a warm place for 5 mins.
- Remove outside leaves and core from cabbage and cut into strips.
- Saute bacon in vegetable oil in a large, pre-heated pot for 2 mins. Add carrot, onion, leek and celery, cook for further 30 secs.
- Add cabbage and cream and cook on high heat, stirring frequently.
- When cream starts to thicken (approx. 5 to 7 mins) reduce to very low heat. Remove breasts from birds by cutting along each side of breast bone.
- Spoon a generous portion of cabbage into the center of each plate. Pour sauce around outside of cabbage. Place a leg and then a breast over cabbage and serve.

NOTE   As with most game, availability of fresh birds varies depending on the season.

BREAST OF CHICKEN WITH LEEK MOUSSELINE & MOREL MUSHROOMS

INGREDIENTS

6 Chicken Breasts
(size 12 with skin on)

24 Baby Leeks
(roots and outside skin removed)

24 Morel Mushrooms

6 Leek Mousselines
(see recipe page 158)

30 gm Butter

30 ml Vegetable Oil

100 gm Unsalted Butter (soft)

200 ml Cream

50 ml Black Truffle Oil

1 teasp Lemon Juice

White Pepper (ground)

BLACK TRUFFLE SAUCE

40 gm Sliced Shallots

750 ml Chicken Stock
(see recipe page 148)

METHOD

- Trim excess skin and fat off chicken breasts.
- Bring shallots and chicken stock to the boil in a heavy pot, reduce by 4/5 (approx. 150 ml), add cream and reduce by 1/3 (approx. 235 ml).
- Strain into a stainless steel bowl and slowly whisk in butter.
- Add truffle oil, lemon juice and season to taste.
- Heat vegetable oil in a heavy pan, cook chicken breasts until well coloured (approx. 12 mins).
- Remove chicken breasts to a warm place and allow to rest.
- Bring 2 litres of salted water to the boil and cook leeks for 2 mins. Remove from heat and slice on an angle.
- Add butter to a heavy pan and lightly saute morels.
- Place a leek mousseline in the center of each plate.
- Slice chicken breasts and rest over mousseline.
- Arrange morels and leeks around outside of plate, sauce lightly and serve.

NOTE If using dried morels, soak overnight in water and drain before using.

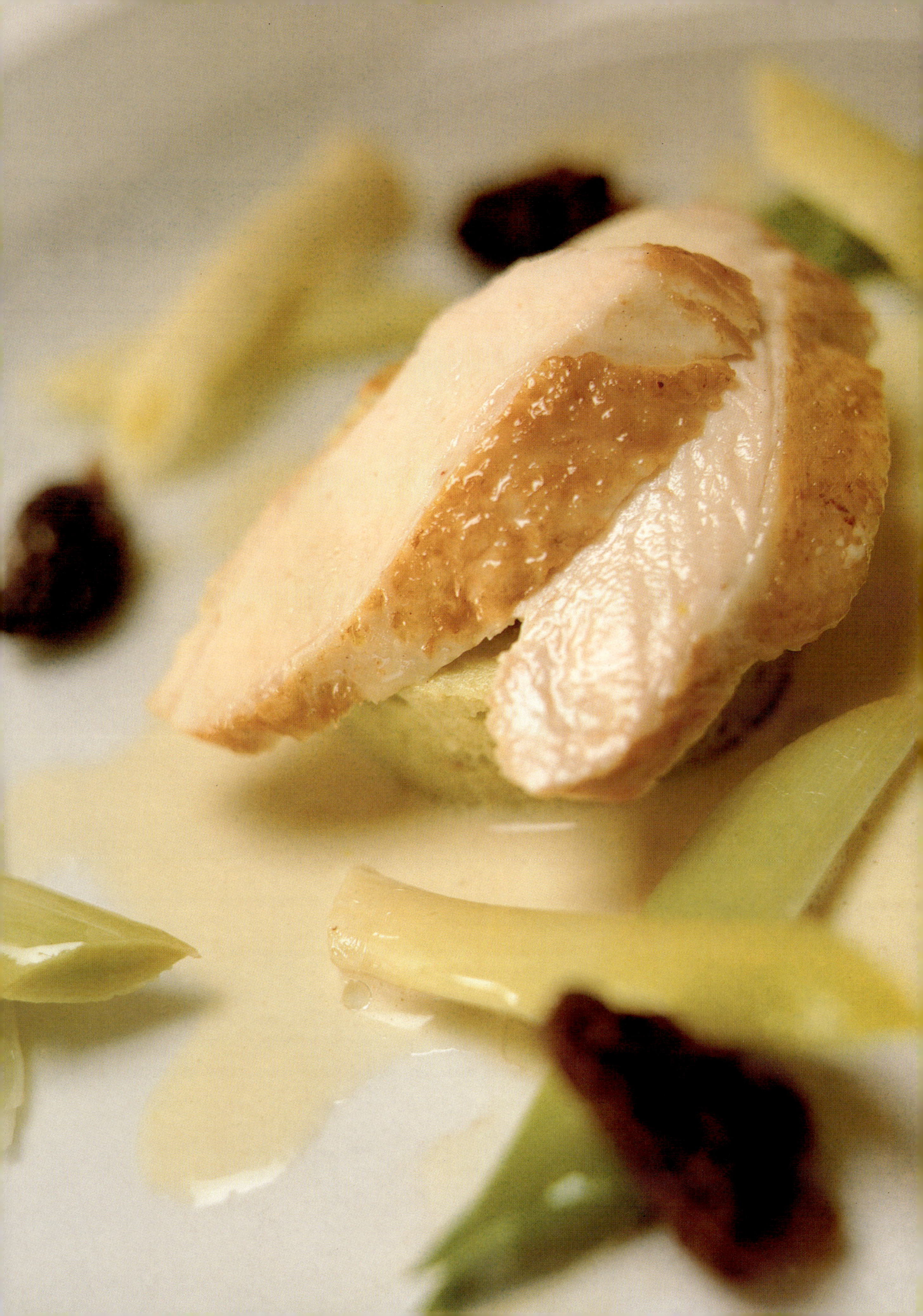

SQUAB PIGEON WITH FOIE GRAS BUTTER

INGREDIENTS
3 x 150 gm Squab Pigeons
60 ml Vegetable Oil
6 small Field Mushrooms
60 gm Foie Gras Pate (diced small)
500 gm Broad Beans
30 gm Butter
Foie Gras Butter
(see recipe page 152)
Chervil

METHOD
- Shell broad beans and blanch in boiling salted water for 2 min.
- Remove from heat and refresh under cold running water.
- When cool remove outside husk from each bean.
- Pre-heat oven and baking tray to 200°C.
- Pour 30 ml vegetable oil into baking tray, roast pigeons breast side down until lightly coloured (approx. 10 mins).
- Turn pigeon and cook breast up for another 5 mins, remove from oven and rest for 10 mins.
- Remove stalks from field mushrooms and saute in a hot pan with 30 ml vegetable oil.
- Warm broad beans gently with butter.
- Place one field mushroom in the center of each plate.
- Scatter broad beans and foie gras dice around outside of plate.
- Carve breasts and legs from pigeons and rest over mushroom.
- Pour sauce around outside of plate, garnish with chervil and serve.

NOTE Squab pigeon is traditionaly served rare. Any game bird can be substituted in this dish.

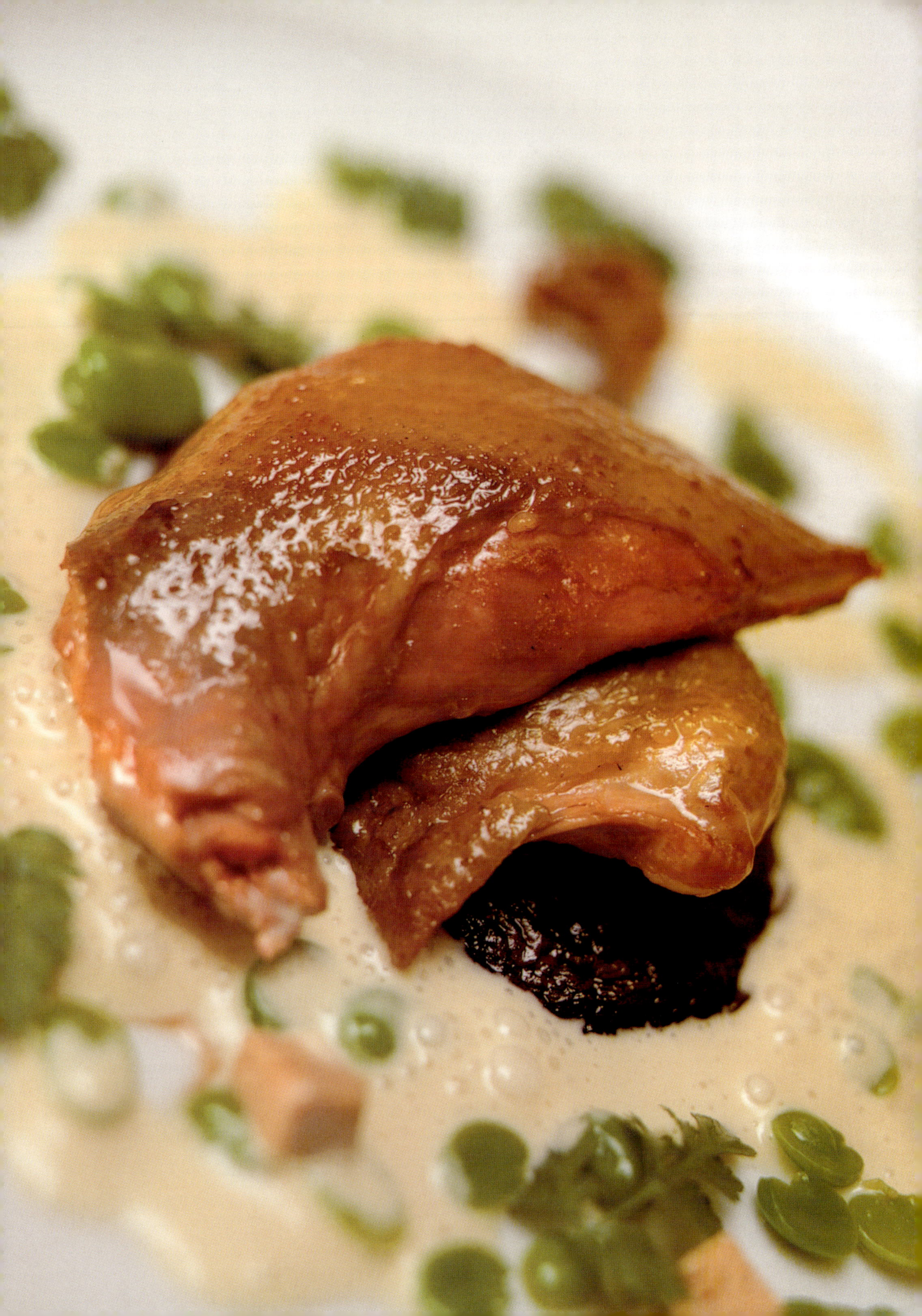

MILK-FED VEAL ON ROESTI WITH WILD MUSHROOMS

INGREDIENTS

6 x 150 gm Veal Cutlets (French trimmed)

36 small Oyster Mushrooms

100 gm Black Fungus (cut into strips)

12 Asparagus Spears (peeled)

6 Baby Leeks (peeled and trimmed)

1 small Black Truffle (thinly sliced)

3 medium Bintje Potatoes (peeled and grated)

300 ml Madeira Sauce (see recipe page 152)

300 ml Vegetable Oil

METHOD

- Pre-heat 250 ml vegetable oil in a heavy based pan on medium heat.
- Rest three egg rings in oil and spoon potato into rings until well filled. Cook until golden brown on both sides. Remove roesti and drain on kitchen paper, then repeat process.
- Pre-heat oven to 180°C and bring 1.5 litres lightly salted water to the boil.
- Pre-heat 30 ml vegetable oil in a heavy based pan on medium heat.
- Seal cutlets in pan until lightly coloured on both sides, remove to oven and cook for 7 mins.
- After 5 mins add roesti potatoes to oven tray.
- Blanch baby leeks in boiling water for 2 mins, add asparagus and cook for further 2 mins. Remove leeks and asparagus from heat and drain.
- Heat 20 ml vegetable oil in a heavy based pan, saute mushrooms and fungus for 1 min.
- Remove roesti and cutlets from oven and place a roesti in the center of each of six plates. Arrange mushrooms around plate and stack asparagus and leeks on one side.
- Drizzle plate lightly with sauce, rest cutlet over roesti, garnish with truffle and serve.

NOTE Australian veal is often much too old. By pre-ordering from a good butcher, smaller and milk-fed meats are obtainable, although more expensive.

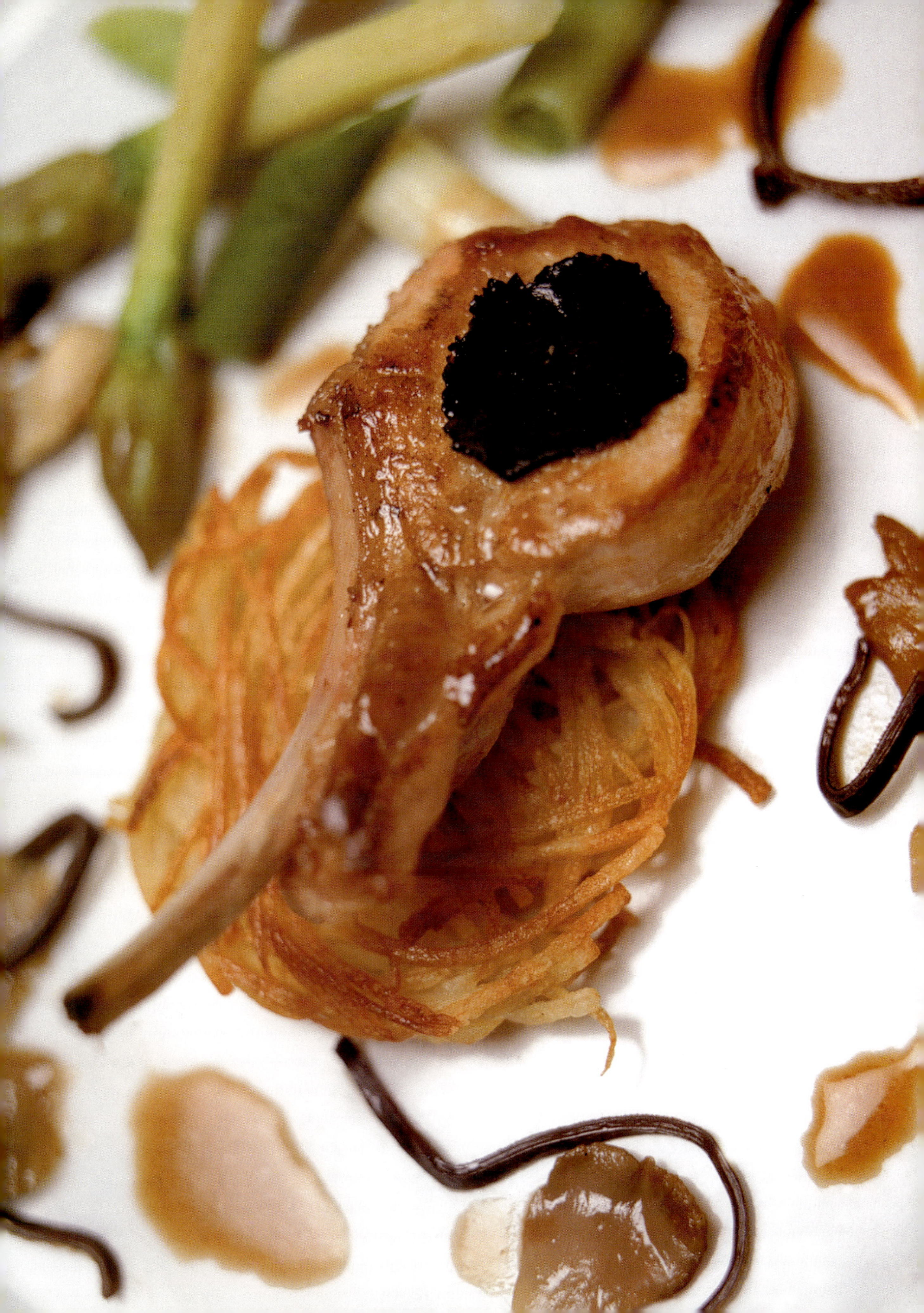

RACK OF SUCKLING PORK WITH ROAST VEGETABLES

INGREDIENTS

2 x 6 bone Suckling Pork Racks (french trimmed)

4 Green Apples (peeled, cored and thinly sliced)

50 gm Butter

1/2 Lemon (juice only)

2 medium Carrots (peeled and cut into thick batons)

2 medium Parsnips (peeled and cut into thick batons)

1 small Sweet Potato (peeled and cut into rounds)

12 small Potatoes (peeled)

18 Shallots (peeled)

100 ml Vegetable Oil

300 ml Chicken Jus (see recipe page 151)

METHOD

- Cook apples in butter with a pinch of salt in a heavy based saucepan on medium heat. When apples are very soft, remove from heat, add lemon juice and puree in a food processor.

- Pre-heat oven and roasting tray to 220°C.

- Score pork skin evenly, rub well with oil and lightly salt. Place racks skin side down in hot tray and cook in oven until skin starts to crackle (approx. 25 mins).

- Turn racks skin side up, add potatoes and reduce oven temperature to 200°C. After 15 mins turn potatoes and add carrots, parsnips and sweet potatoes, return to oven.

- After 10 mins turn vegetables and add shallots, return to oven for 10 to 15 mins.

- Remove racks and vegetables from tray and rest in a warm place. Pour excess fat from tray and discard.

- Add chicken jus to tray and bring to the boil on stove top, scrape sediment from base into sauce, simmer for 1 min and strain.

- Divide vegetables evenly between six plates.

- Carve racks, skin side down, into individual cutlets and rest over vegetables.

- Spoon sauce around plates. Serve apple sauce separately.

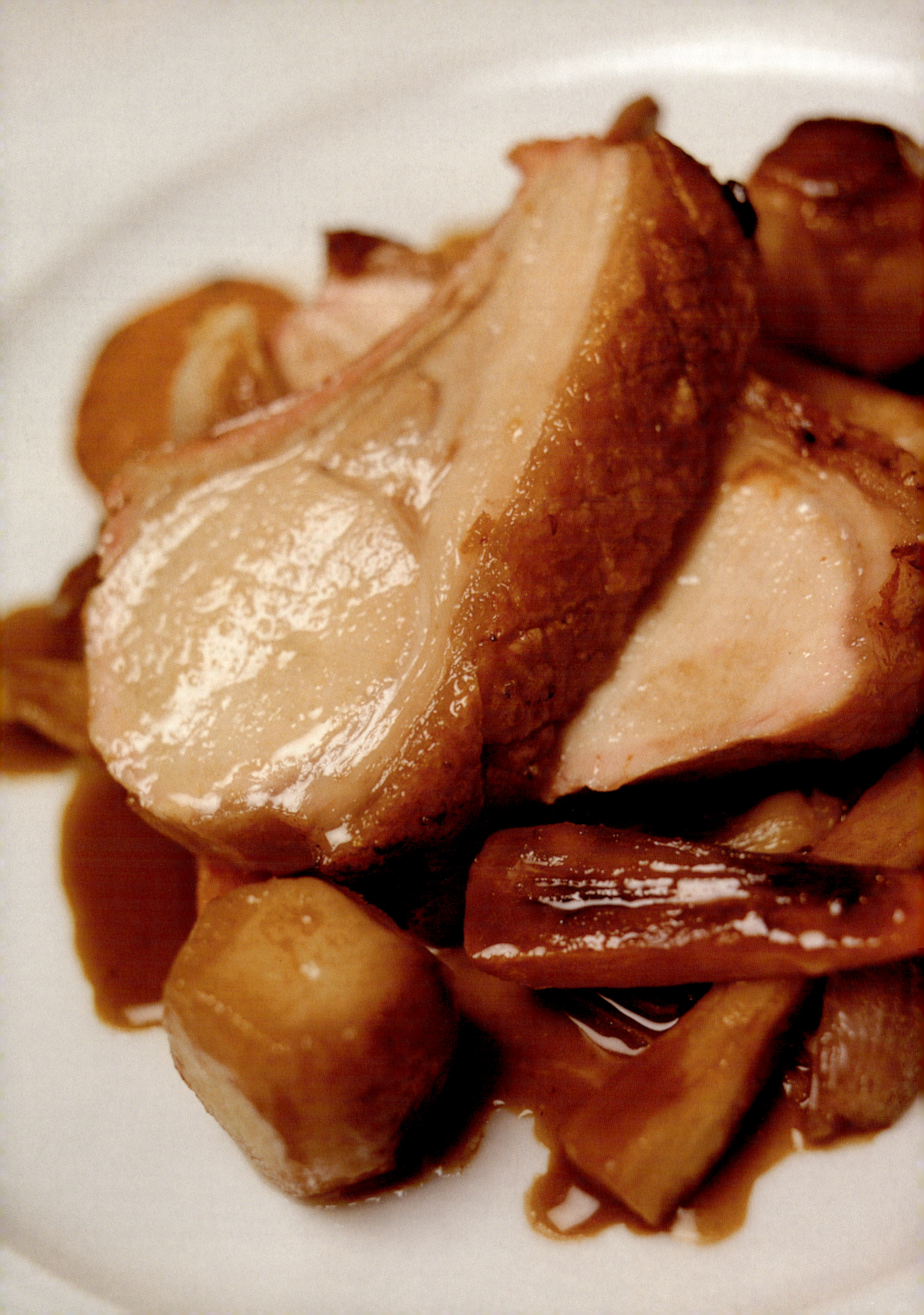

LOIN OF LAMB WITH GARDEN PEAS & PARSNIP MASH

INGREDIENTS

6 x 180 gm Lamb Loins
(fat and sinew removed)

2 Parsnips
(peeled and cut into large batons)

12 Scallions

180 gm Garden Peas (shelled)

300 ml Lamb Jus
(see recipe page 150)

160 ml Vegetable Oil

100 gm Potatoes
(peeled and chopped)

250 ml Milk

50 gm Butter

50 ml Cream

PARSNIP MASH

500 gm Parsnips
(peeled and chopped)

METHOD

- Bring parsnips, potatoes, milk, 500 ml water and 1 teasp salt to the boil in a heavy based pot. Cook for 20 mins.

- Remove from heat and drain, pass through a mouli or blend in a food processor. Pre-heat oven to 180°C

- Heat 10 ml vegetable oil in a heavy based pan on high heat. Seal loins until well coloured, remove to oven and cook for 7 mins.

- Heat 150 ml vegetable oil in a heavy based pan. Shallow fry parsnips until light gold and crisp, drain on kitchen paper.

- Re-heat parsnip mash with butter, cream and season to taste.

- Bring 1.5 litres salted water to the boil, blanch scallions in boiling water, after 2 mins add peas and cook for further 2 mins then drain.

- Spoon parsnip mash into center of six plates and arrange vegetables around outside of plate.

- Spoon sauce over parsnip mash and vegetables. Slice loins into thirds, rest over mash and serve.

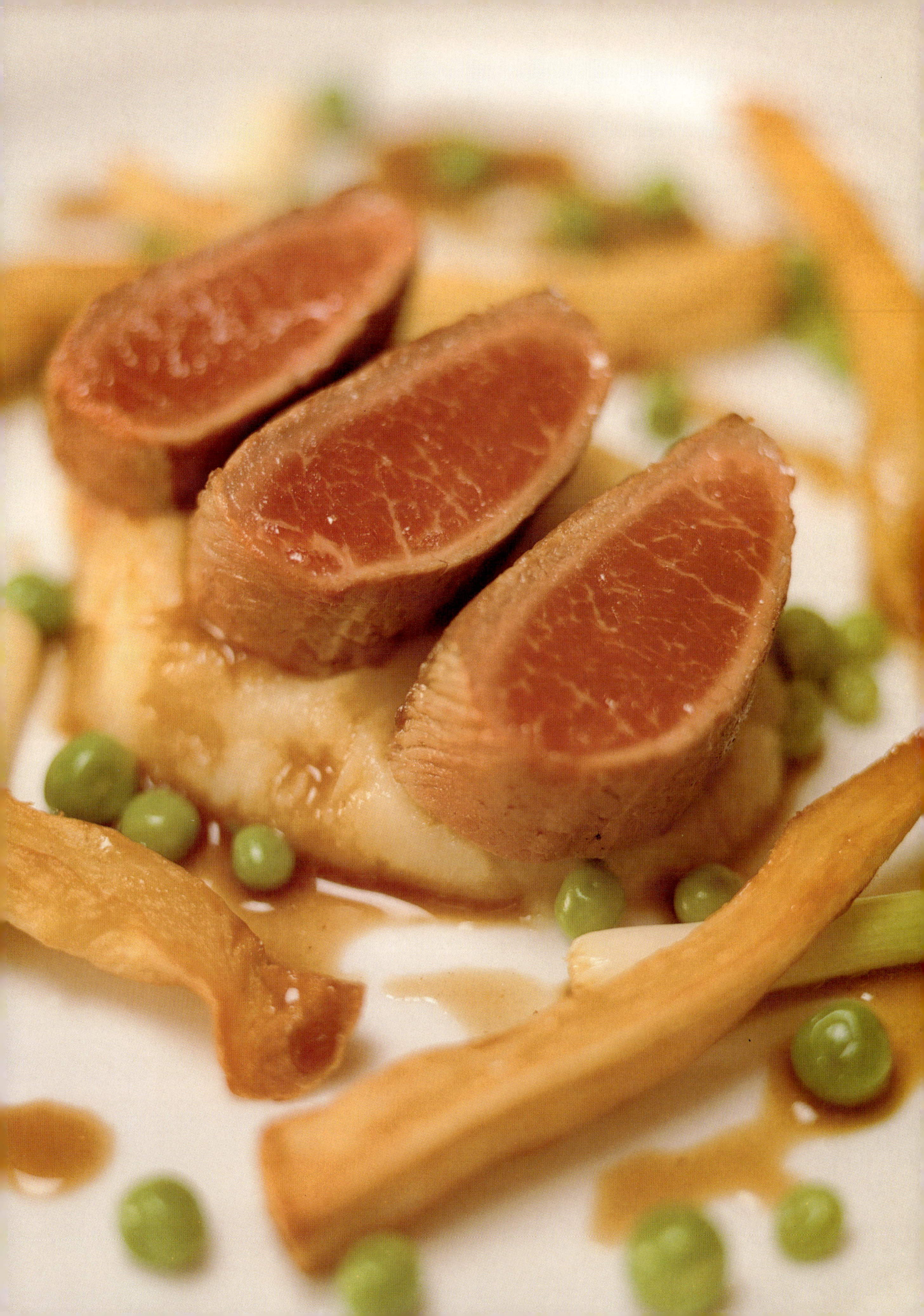

FILLET OF BEEF WITH BORDELAISE SAUCE

INGREDIENTS

12 x 100 gm Eye Fillet Steaks (well trimmed)

18 slices Bone Marrow

18 cloves Roast Garlic (see recipe page 159)

18 Roast Shallots (see recipe page 159)

6 New Potatoes (peeled and sliced)

70 ml Vegetable Oil

400 ml Bordelaise Sauce (see recipe page 152)

METHOD

- Season steaks lightly with salt and pepper.
- Heat 20 ml vegetable oil in a heavy based pan on high heat.
- Seal steaks well and allow to cook for 3 mins each side.
- Remove steaks and rest in a warm place for 5 mins.
- Heat 50 ml vegetable oil on medium heat and saute potatoes until golden brown.
- Warm shallots and garlic on a lightly oiled tray in oven for 5 mins. Add marrow after 4 mins.
- Place 2 steaks in the centre of each plate and arrange potatoes, garlic and shallots around.
- Cover steaks well with sauce, then rest marrow over meat and serve.

NOTE Beef marrow can be pre-ordered from good butchers. If purchasing marrow bones, ask your butcher to split the bones. All marrow should be soaked in water overnight before using.

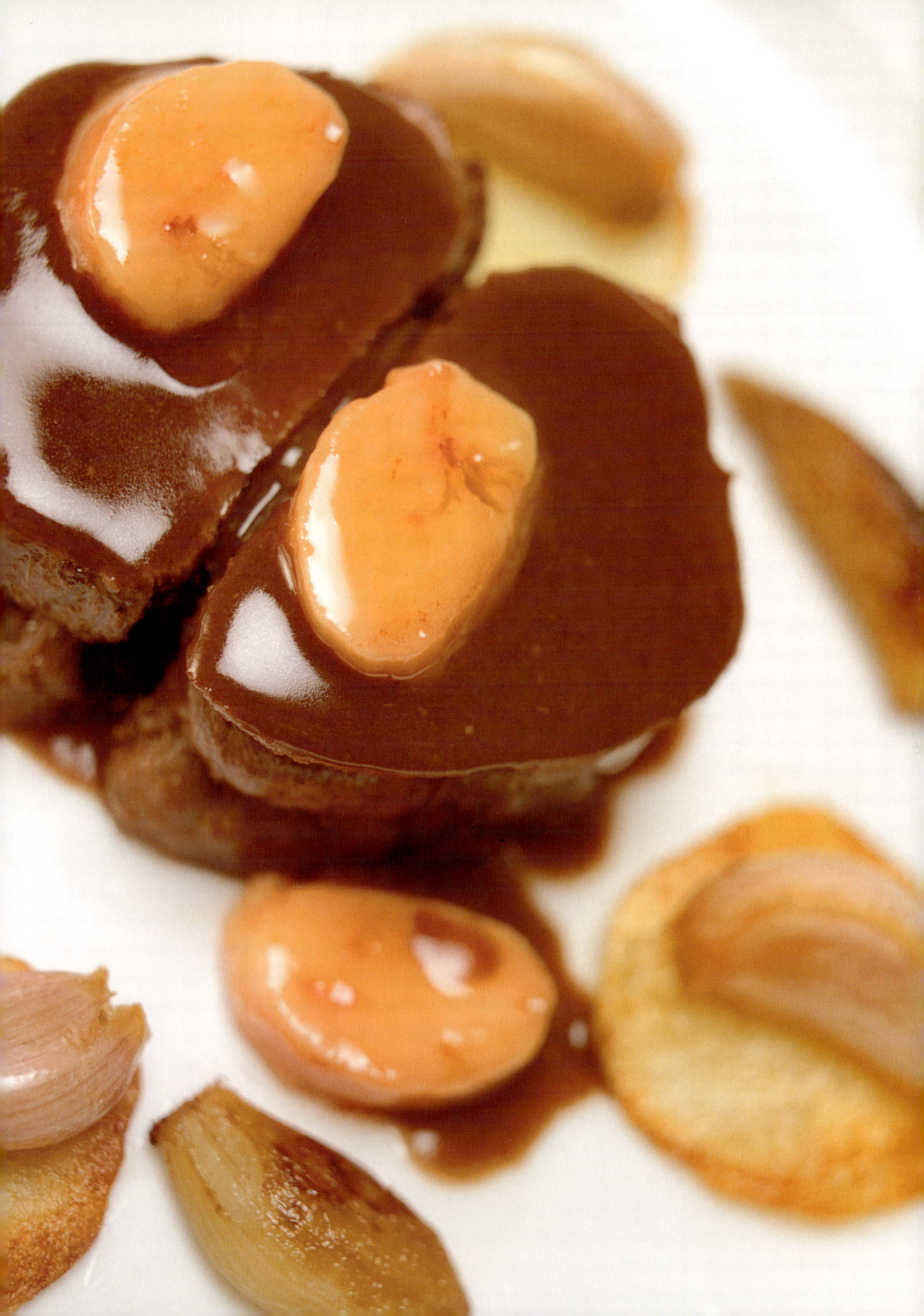

TRADITIONAL STEAK & KIDNEY PIE

INGREDIENTS

500 gm Puff Pastry
(see recipe page 155)

1 kg Chuck Steak
(sinew removed and cubed)

250 gm Veal Kidneys
(cleaned and cubed)

250 gm Button Mushrooms
(cut in half)

2 large Brown Onions (sliced)

1 litre Demi Glaze
(see recipe page 149)

375 ml Stout

25 ml Worcestershire Sauce

1 Egg (whisked)

METHOD

- Sear separately, chuck steak, kidneys and mushrooms in a very hot pan until coloured. Drain and retain liquid for later use.
- Saute onions in a large braising or roasting pan until coloured, add stout and reduce by 2/3.
- Add demi glaze, Worcestershire sauce, chuck steak and reserved liquid.
- Braise on low heat for 3 hrs, add kidneys and mushrooms then remove from heat.
- Allow to cool, divide into pie dishes, cover with pastry, brush with egg. Cook in a moderate oven until pastry is golden brown.

NOTE

Commercial puff pastry will work well in this dish. Puff pastry can also be pre-ordered from some good pastry shops. Steak and kidney pie should be served with plenty of potato or parsnip mash and fresh garden peas.

PEPPERED VENISON & BEETROOT RELISH

INGREDIENTS

6 x 150 gm Venison Loins

170 ml Vegetable Oil

300 ml Venison Jus (see recipe page 150)

Spaetzli (see recipe page 156)

RELISH

4 large Beetroots (peeled and coarsely grated)

2 tblsp Horseradish (grated)

1 Salad Onion (thinly sliced)

200 ml Red Wine Vinegar

2 desp Castor Sugar

1/2 Orange (zest and juice)

50 gm Dried Currants

1 pinch Nutmeg (fresh grated)

1/2 Bay Leaf

METHOD

- Combine all ingredients for relish in a heavy based pot.
- Bring to the boil then reduce to low heat. Stir frequently and cook gently until 'jammy' (approx. 1hr).
- Cool, remove bay leaf and refrigerate overnight in a sealed container.
- Heat 20 ml vegetable oil in a heavy based pan until very hot. Sear venison until well sealed (3 to 4 mins each side), remove from heat and rest in a warm place for 5 mins. Venison should be quite rare when served.
- Heat remaining oil in a heavy based pan and saute spaetzli until crisp (approx. 5 mins). Drain well on kitchen paper.
- Warm beetroot relish gently on stove and spoon into the center of each plate. Pour jus around relish and scatter spaetzli around plate.
- Carve venison into thirds, lay over relish and serve.

RIB OF BEEF WITH BEARNAISE SAUCE

INGREDIENTS 6 x 500 gm Beef Ribs

18 Scallions

REDUCTION

500 ml Tarragon Vinegar

100 gm Shallots (sliced)

250 ml White Wine (riesling or other unwooded wine)

2 desp Black Pepper (ground)

1/4 bunch Tarragon (chopped)

1 Bay Leaf

SAUCE

2 desp Bearnaise Reduction

4 Egg Yolks

300 ml Unsalted Butter (clarified)

1 desp White Wine Vinegar

1 pinch Cayenne Pepper

2 pinches Salt

2 desp Water (warm)

1 tblsp Mixed Herbs (chopped tarragon, parsley, chervil)

1/4 Lemon (juice only)

METHOD

- Bring all reduction ingredients to the boil in a stainless pot and reduce by 1/2. Cool and store in refrigerator.

- Place cooled reduction, egg yolks, vinegar, salt, cayenne and water in a stainless steel bowl. Whisk constantly in a hot bain-marie until thick enough to leave a trail on the side of the bowl for three seconds (approx. 5 mins).

- Remove bowl from heat and slowly whisk in clarified butter. Strain sauce then add chopped herbs.

- Trim excess fat and sinew from beef. Remove outside leaves from scallions and cut to 10 cm length.

- Pre-heat oven and roasting dish to 220°C. Seal ribs in a very hot pan on stove until well coloured. Remove to oven in roasting dish.

- Turn ribs after 5 mins and add scallions to dish. Cook for further 5 mins and remove ribs. Allow to rest in a warm place for 5 mins.

- Place ribs on plates, remove scallions from oven and arrange beside ribs.

- Spoon Bearnaise over ribs and serve.

NOTE Always use a reputable butcher when sourcing meat for this dish. Some hand-cut chips or potato mash makes a great accompaniment.

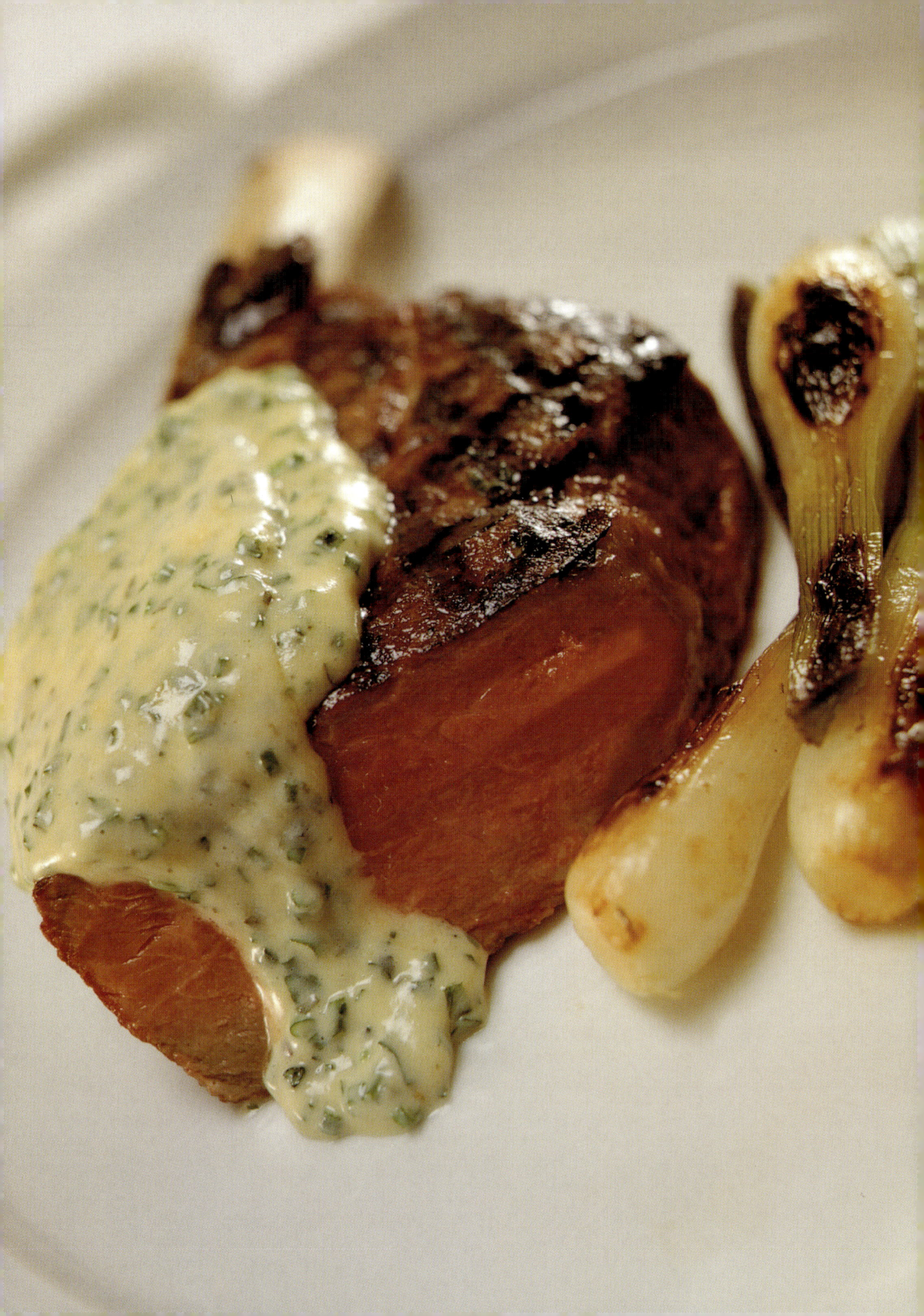

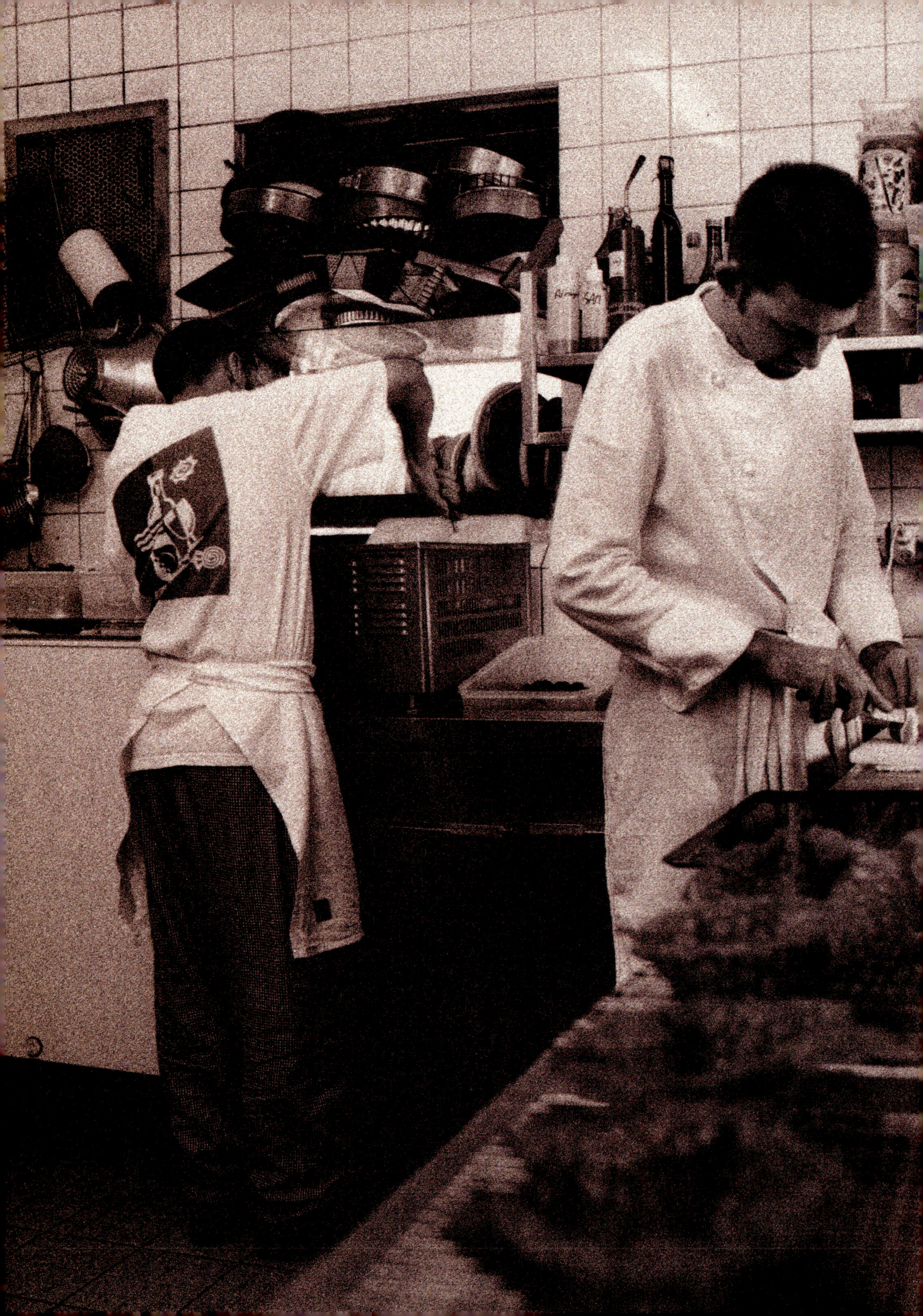

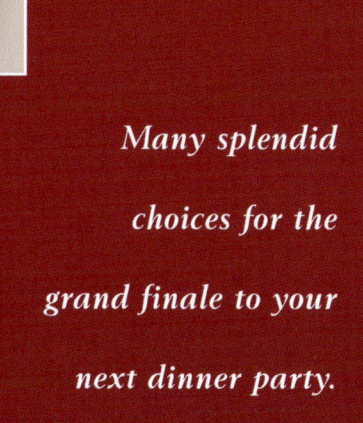

DESSERTS

Many splendid choices for the grand finale to your next dinner party.

VANILLA BEAN CREME BRULEE WITH ARMAGNAC PRUNES

INGREDIENTS

BRULEE

300 ml Cream

8 Egg Yolks

100 gm Castor Sugar

2 Vanilla Beans

ARMAGNAC PRUNES

18 large Prunes

100 ml Armagnac

200 ml Stock Syrup
(see recipe page 162)

1 Cinnamon Quill

GARNISH

6 Tuile Biscuits
(see recipe page 163)

Castor Sugar

Icing Sugar

METHOD

- Split vanilla beans lengthways.
- Heat cream and vanilla beans gently (do not boil).
- Whisk egg yolks and sugar together.
- Add cream slowly to egg mix whisking continuously. Heat gently over a double boiler until mix reaches a custard consistency (25 to 30 mins).
- Place bowl over ice to cool, remove vanilla beans after scraping out seeds into mix and stir gently to remove all air bubbles.
- Spoon mix into ramekins and allow to set.
- Bring sugar syrup and cinnamon quill to the boil in a large pot, add prunes and simmer for five minutes. Remove from heat and stir in armagnac, allow to cool then store in a sterile container in refrigerator until needed.
- Sprinkle castor sugar lightly over the top of ramekins. Spray with a little water and burn sugar with a blow torch until golden brown.
- Cool then serve with prunes and biscuit (dusted with icing sugar) on the side.

NOTE

The longer that prunes can be left in syrup the better the flavours will become. If no blow torch is available, pack ramekins in ice and place under a very hot grill. Except for burning the sugar, all of this dish can be prepared in advance.

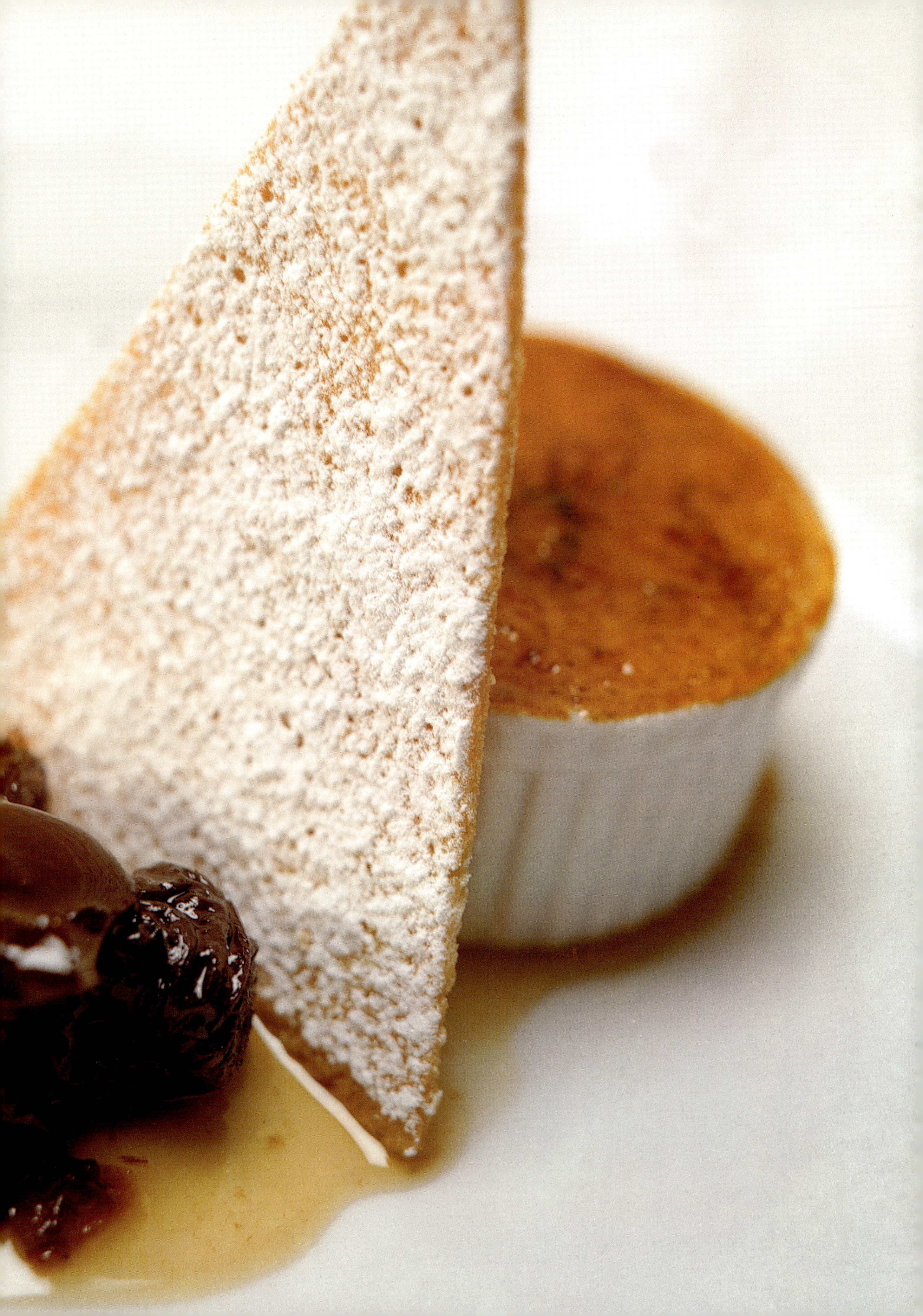

WHITE CHOCOLATE BRULEE WITH RASPBERRIES

INGREDIENTS 100 gm White Chocolate (grated)

300 ml Cream

8 Egg Yolks

100 ml Castor Sugar

2 Vanilla Beans

GARNISH

6 Tuile Biscuits
(see recipe page 163)

Castor Sugar

2 punnets Fresh Raspberries

Icing Sugar

METHOD
- Split vanilla beans lengthways.
- Heat cream and vanilla beans gently (do not boil).
- Whisk together egg yolks and sugar, add cream slowly to egg mix whisking continuously.
- Heat gently over a double boiler until mix reaches a custard consistency (25 to 30 mins), stir in white chocolate until disolved.
- Place bowl over ice to cool, remove vanilla beans after scraping out seeds into mix and stir gently to remove all air bubbles.
- Spoon mix into ramekins and allow to set. Lightly sprinkle castor sugar over the top of ramekins.
- Spray with a little water and burn sugar with a blow torch until golden brown. Stack raspberries on side of plate and dust heavily with icing sugar.
- Place brulees and tuile biscuits on plate and serve.

NOTE If no blow torch is available, pack ramekins in ice and place under a very hot grill. Apart from raspberries other summer berries or stone fruits will compliment this dish. Except for burning the sugar, all of this dish can be prepared in advance.

LEMON SOUFFLE WITH LEMON MYRTLE ICE CREAM

INGREDIENTS

300 gm Egg Whites
(whites of approx. 9 large eggs)

300 gm Castor Sugar

1 Lemon (zest only)

5 Lemons (juice only)

Unsalted Butter

extra Castor Sugar

Lemon Myrtle Ice Cream
(see recipe page 160)

METHOD

- Reduce lemon juice by 3/4 on medium heat in a small, heavy based pot and allow to cool.
- Pre-heat oven to 180°C, butter souffle dishes and lightly coat with castor sugar. Whisk egg whites in mixing bowl with 1/2 castor sugar.
- Add remaining sugar slowly when mix forms soft peaks. Continue whisking until soft peaks form again and stop whisking.
- Fold zest and juice gently into mix then spoon into dishes. Fill dishes to the top and remove excess until level.
- Run thumb around rim of each dish forming a 1/2 cm ring, this will allow souffle to rise evenly.
- Place souffles on a flat tray on bottom shelf of oven and cook for 12 to 14 mins.
- Remove souffles from oven when well risen and top is lightly coloured.
- Dust with icing sugar and serve with lemon myrtle ice cream.

NOTE

Lemon juice is reduced not only for flavour intensity, but also to break down the acids that would curdle the egg whites.

CHOCOLATE SOUFFLE WITH WHITE CHOCOLATE ICE CREAM

INGREDIENTS 30 gm Cocoa Powder (sifted)

300 gm Castor Sugar

300 gm Egg Whites
(whites of approx. 9 large eggs)

Unsalted Butter

Extra Castor Sugar

White Chocolate Ice Cream
(see recipe page 161)

METHOD
- Pre-heat oven to 170°C.
- Butter inside of souffle dishes and coat lightly with castor sugar.
- Whisk egg whites in mixing bowl with 1/2 castor sugar. When mix forms soft peaks slowly add remaining sugar.
- Continue whisking until soft peaks form again and stop whisking. Fold cocoa powder gently into mix and spoon into dishes.
- Fill dishes to the top and remove excess until level. Run thumb around rim of each dish forming a 1/2 cm ring, this will allow souffle to rise evenly.
- Place souffles on a flat tray on bottom shelf of oven and cook until risen and lightly coloured (approx. 12 to 14 mins).
- Remove souffles from oven and dust with cocoa powder, serve with white chocolate ice cream.

NOTE Premium quality cocoa powder will give best results in this dish. Cooking times may vary depending on your oven.

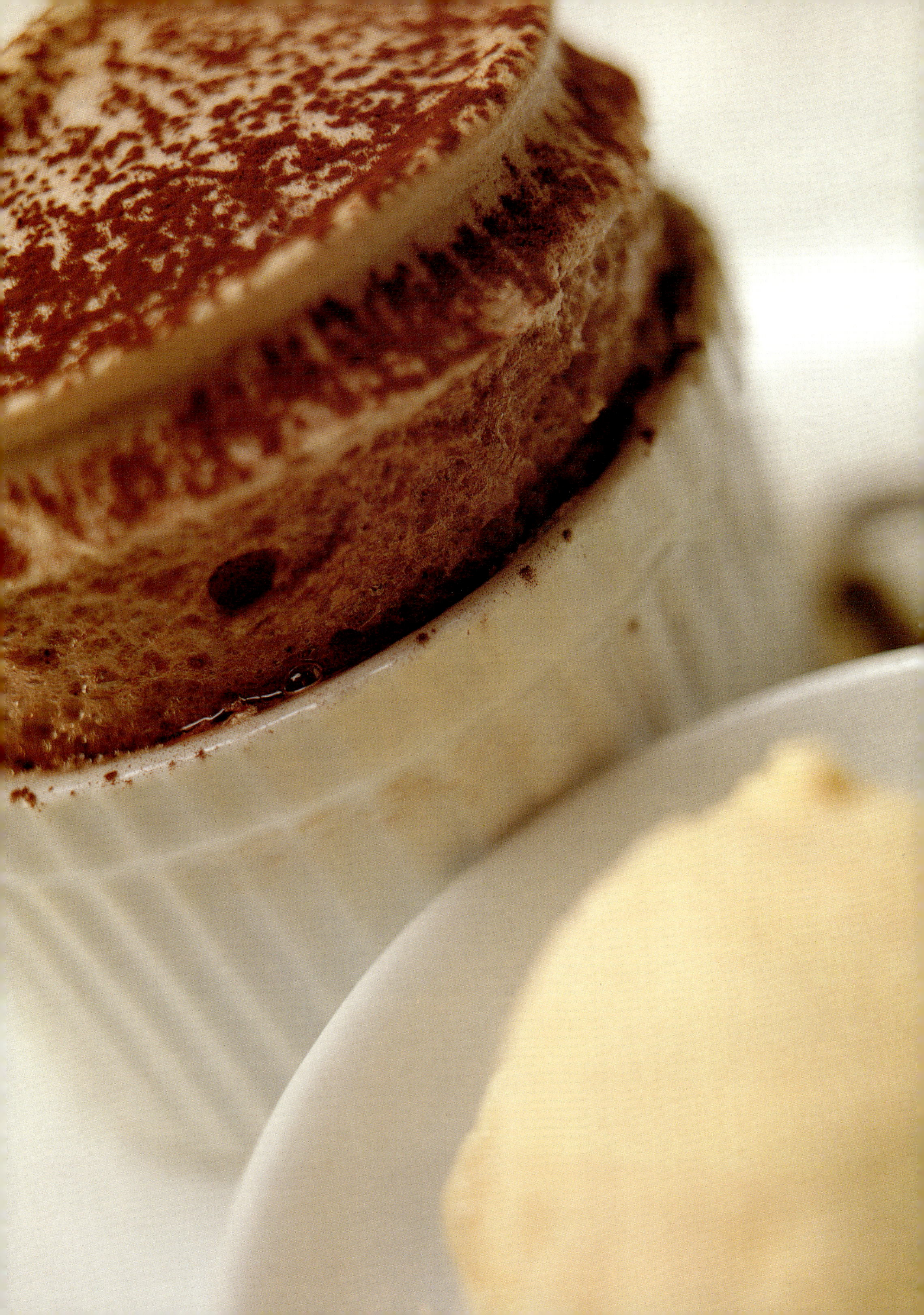

DARK CHOCOLATE SORBET WITH BLACK CHERRIES

INGREDIENTS

350 gm Black Cherries (pitted)

1 litre Stock Syrup
(see recipe page 162)

1 Cinamon Quill

6 Tuile Biscuits
(see recipe page 163)

SORBET

200 gm Dark Chocolate

300 gm Castor Sugar

METHOD

- Bring stock syrup and cinnamon quill to the boil in a medium pot.
- Remove from heat, add cherries, allow to cool and refrigerate in a sealed container.
- Bring 500 ml water and castor sugar to the boil in a small pot. Remove from heat and allow to cool for 10 mins.
- Chop or grate chocolate roughly and stir into syrup until smooth.
- Freeze mixture in an ice cream maker or round bowl, stirring every ten minutes until frozen.
- Scoop sorbet into base of dessert bowl and spoon cherries over.
- Garnish with tuile biscuit and serve.

NOTE

Chocolate sorbet makes a rich but refreshing finish to a summer meal.

PEACH & RASPBERRY TRIFLE

INGREDIENTS 3 ripe Peaches (peeled and stoned)

1 punnet Raspberries

1 Vanilla Sponge

250 gm Mascarpone

200 ml Stock Syrup
(see recipe page 162)

30 ml Grand Marnier

150 ml Raspberry Puree
(see recipe page 162)

Icing Sugar

METHOD
- Cut peaches vertically into twelfths, cut sponge into three, 2 cm thick slices.
- Shape first piece of sponge to neatly cover base of terrine mould.
- Mix Grand Marnier and stock syrup then brush 1/3 over sponge.
- Spread 1/3 mascarpone over sponge and cover with 1/2 sliced peaches.
- Cut next piece of sponge to shape and lay firmly over peaches.
- Brush with next 1/3 stock syrup and cover with next 1/3 mascarpone.
- Cover with remaining peaches and 1/2 raspberries.
- Cut remaining piece of sponge to shape and lay firmly over fruit. Brush with remaining syrup and cover with remaining mascarpone.
- Garnish with remaining raspberries, dust with icing sugar and serve with raspberry puree.

NOTE This summer dessert can be made earlier on the day of use.

RED WINE POACHED PEARS WITH RED WINE ICE CREAM

INGREDIENTS 6 ripe Pears (peeled and cored)

750 ml Stock Syrup
(see recipe page 162)

750 ml Red Wine

1 Cinnamon Quill

4 Cloves

1/2 Bay Leaf

Red Wine Ice Cream
(see recipe page 161)

METHOD
- Bring stock syrup, wine and spices to the boil in a large pot. Add pears and reduce heat to simmer, cook until soft (approx. 10 to 15 min).
- Remove from heat and cool. Remove pears from liquid and place in a small container, cover with 1/3 of liquid.
- Strain remaining liquid into a small pot and reduce on high heat until 1/3 remains. Remove from heat, and cool.
- Place a pear in the centre of each plate and lightly cover with red wine syrup. Rest a scoop of ice cream beside each pear and serve.

NOTE This dish can be prepared up to two days in advance, but pears and ice cream taste better when prepared on the day they are served.

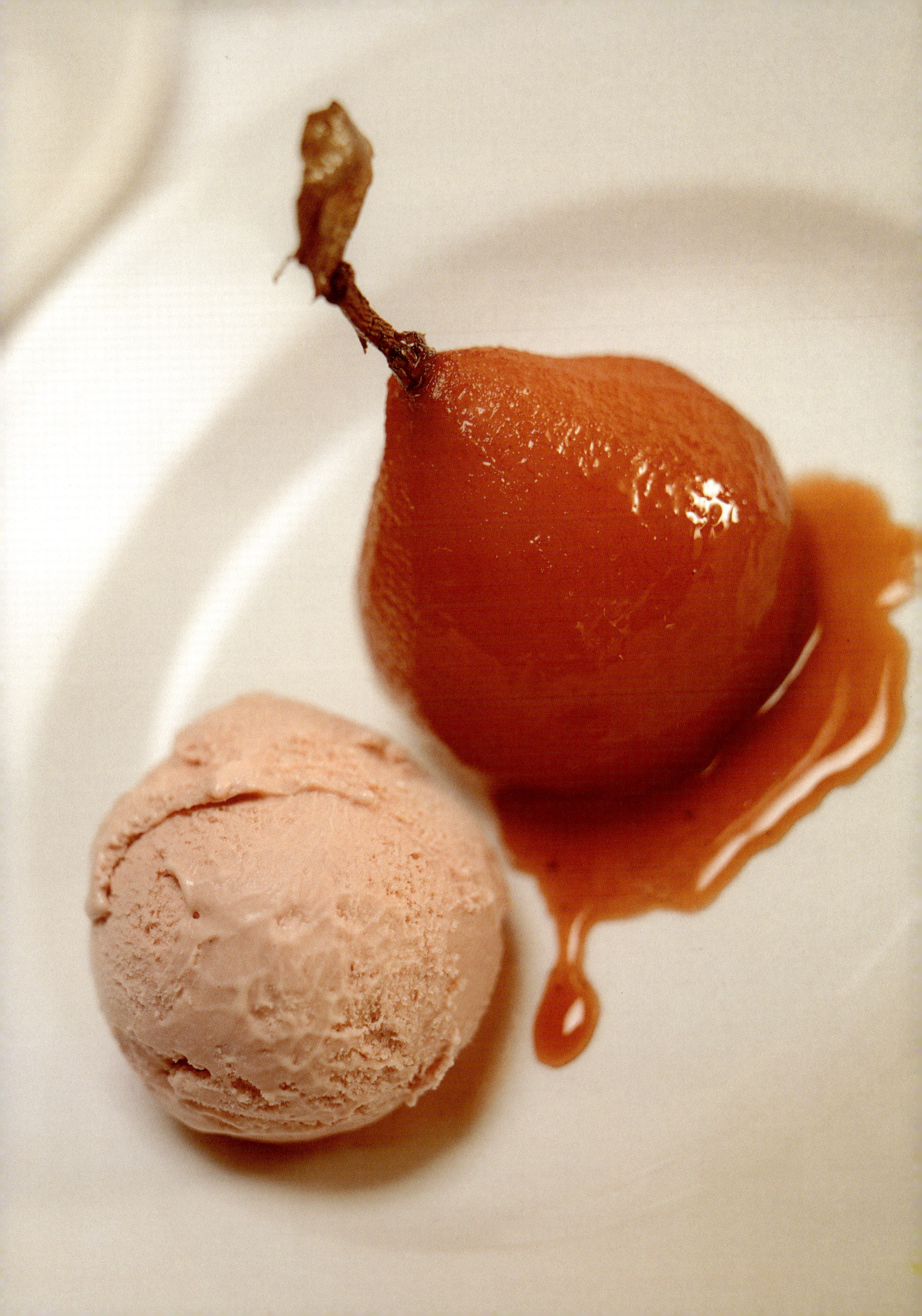

MANGO TART & LIME CREAM

INGREDIENTS

3 Bowen Mangoes (ripe)

Sable Pastry
(see recipe page 163)

50 ml Creme Anglaise
(see recipe page 162)

200 ml Double Cream

1 Lime (zest only)

2 Limes (juice only)

Castor Sugar (to glaze mangoes)

PASSIONFRUIT SYRUP

150 gm Castor Sugar

50 ml Water

4 Passionfruit (pulp only)

1 Lime (juice only)

METHOD

- Roll out sable pastry to 1/2 cm thickness and carefully line six buttered, 8 cm tart tins. Rest pastry for 15 mins.
- Prick pastry with a fork and bake blind in a 180°C pre-heated oven for 15 mins.
- Bring sugar for syrup, water and passionfruit pulp to the boil in a heavy based pot on medium heat, cook for 5 mins, remove from heat and strain.
- When cool, add lime juice and store at room temperature.
- Slice cheeks from mangoes and peel. Shape cheeks to fit tartlets with knife or pastry cutter.
- Trim remaining flesh from seed and dice finely. Combine with creme anglaise, double cream, lime juice and zest.
- Sprinkle mango cheeks lightly with castor sugar. Glaze with a blow torch or cook under a hot grill until lightly coloured.
- Lay tart shells on six plates, 2/3 fill with cream mix and rest mango cheeks over cream.
- Drizzle passionfruit syrup around tart and serve.

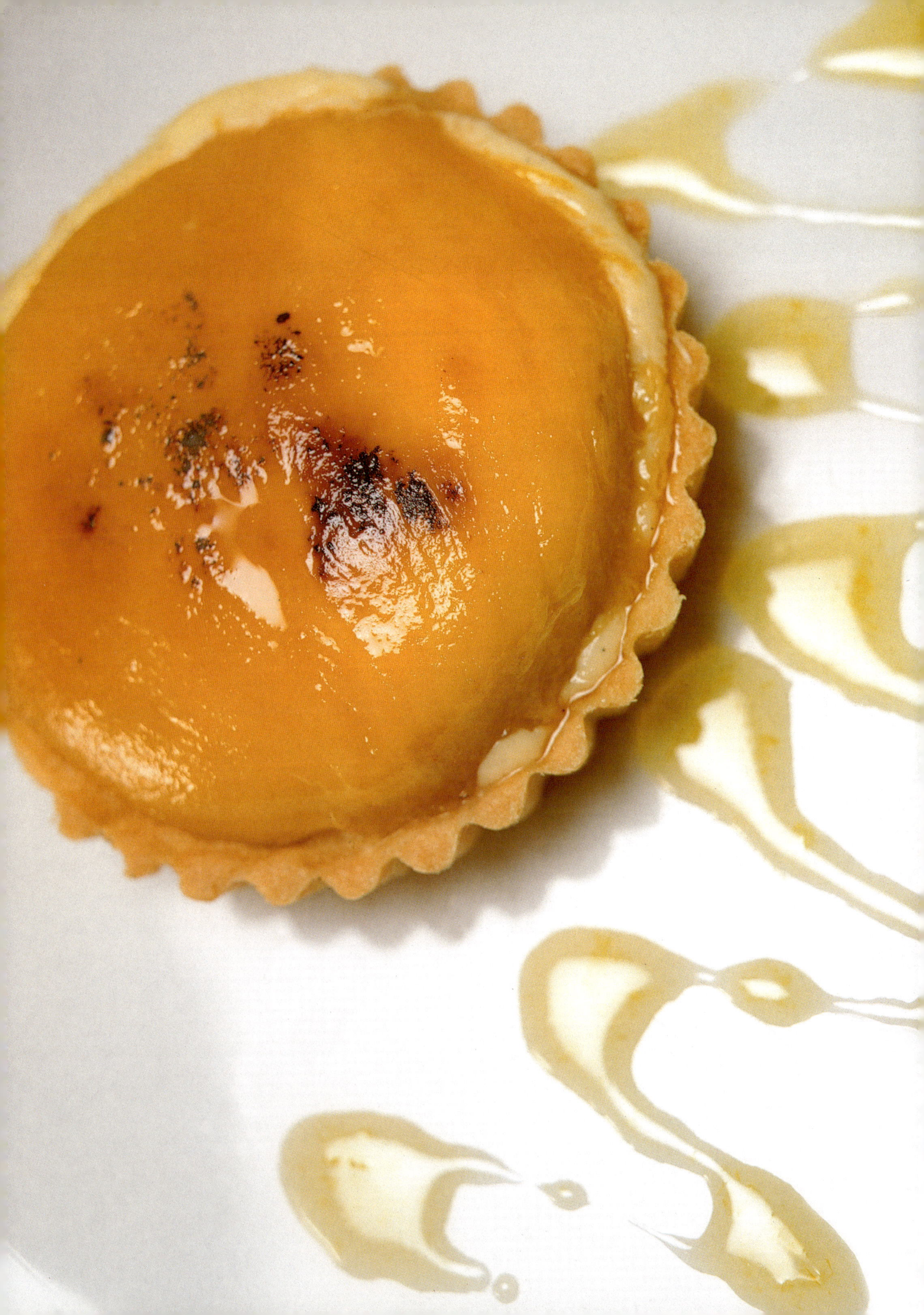

BRANDY SNAPS WITH SUMMER BERRIES

INGREDIENTS
100 gm Butter
160 gm Icing Sugar
100 gm Plain Flour
80 gm Golden Syrup
1 pinch Ginger (powdered)
Vanilla Bean Ice Cream
(see recipe page 160)

1 small punnet Raspberries
1 small punnet Blueberries
1 small punnet Strawberries
1 small punnet Mulberries
1 small punnet Cape Gooseberries
Extra Icing Sugar

METHOD

- Combine butter, icing sugar, flour and ginger in a food processor. Add golden syrup and mix until a smooth, thick paste.

- Pre-heat oven to 180°C. Place a generous dessertspoon of mix at either end of a well-buttered biscuit tray (mix will spread approx. 10 cm when cooking).

- Cook until biscuits are a deep golden brown (approx. 6 to 10 min). Remove tray from oven and rest for 1 min.

- Lift biscuits from tray with a large spatula and rest over up-turned coffee cups to create basket shape. Repeat process to make remaining baskets.

- When cool, store in an airtight container in a cool, dry place.

- Remove any stems from berries and cut strawberries in half.

- Place a brandy snap in the centre of each plate and carefully rest a generous scoop of vanilla bean ice cream in the bottom of each basket.

- Arrange berries over ice cream, dust heavily with icing sugar and serve.

NOTE

Brandy snaps can be made earlier on day of use. Some practice at making baskets is advised before serving at a dinner party.

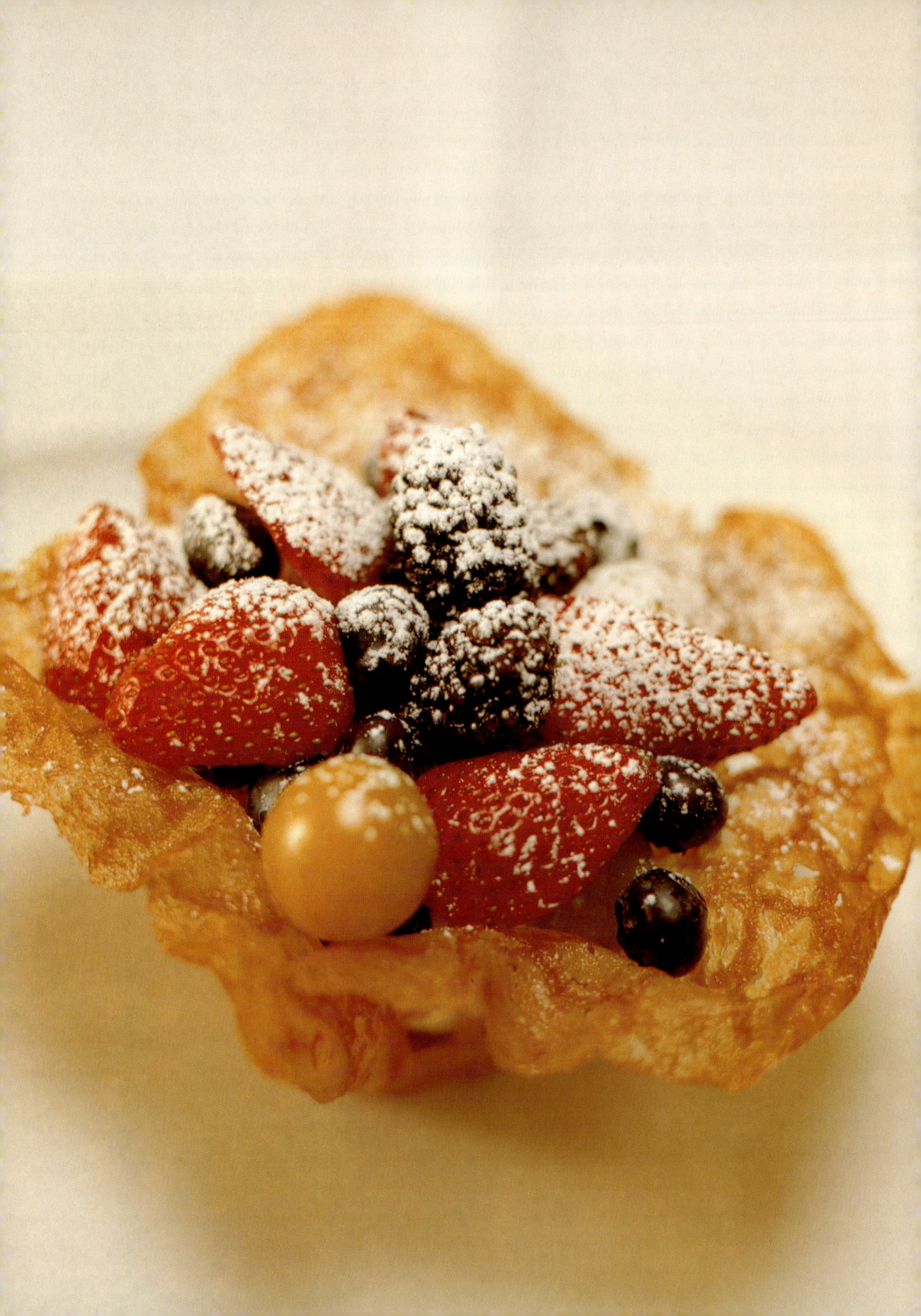

LEMON CREPES WITH BLACK SAMBUCCA ICE CREAM

INGREDIENTS

Black Sambucca Ice Cream (see recipe page 160)

CREPES

125 gm Plain Flour (sifted)

250 ml Milk

25 gm Unsalted Butter (melted)

25 gm Castor Sugar

1 Egg

1 Lemon (zest only)

100 ml Vegetable Oil

LEMON SYRUP

400 ml Stock Syrup (see recipe page 162)

3 Lemons (juice only)

GARNISH

50 ml Black Sambucca

6 Lemon Wedges

extra Castor Sugar

Candied Zest (see recipe page 162)

METHOD

- Whisk milk, butter, sugar, egg and lemon zest in a medium bowl.
- Add flour slowly to make a smooth batter, cover bowl with cling wrap and rest in a cool place for 2 hrs.
- Bring stock syrup to the boil and keep warm.
- Brush a heated crepe pan with vegetable oil. Spoon enough batter into pan to lightly cover base.
- Cook until base is lightly browned and flip crepe, cook second side lightly and turn out on to a warm plate.
- Sprinkle crepe lightly with extra castor sugar and fold into quarters. Cover crepes with a towel to keep warm.
- Repeat process to make 18 crepes.
- Warm six dessert bowls in oven.
- Add lemon juice to stock syrup. Arrange crepes in bowls and cover with lemon syrup. Rest a scoop of sambucca ice cream beside crepes.
- Drizzle ice cream lightly with sambucca, garnish crepes with candied zest and serve.

NOTE Crepes can be pre-made and warmed in lemon syrup.

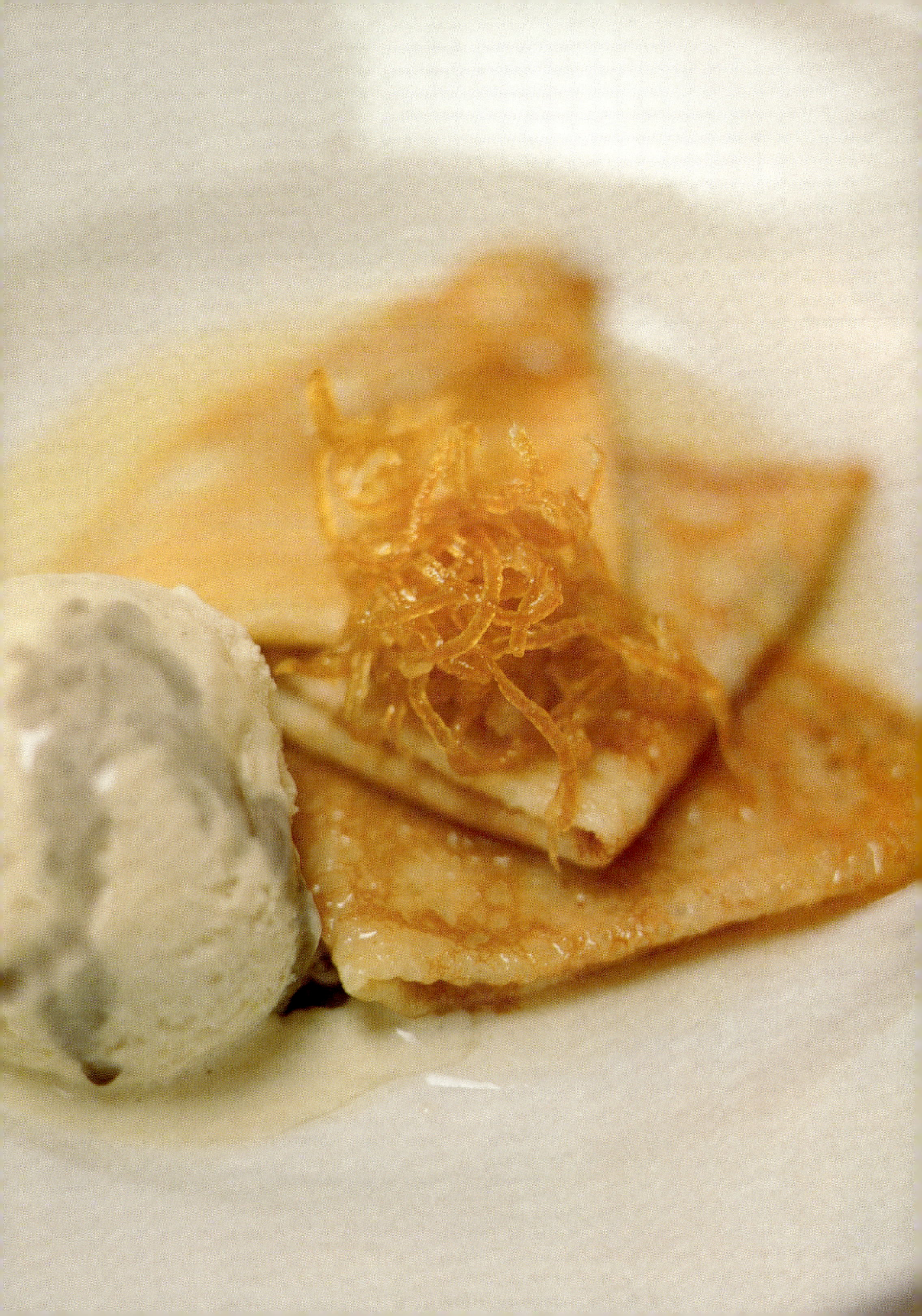

BITTER-SWEET CHOCOLATE TART WITH CITRUS SALAD

INGREDIENTS

500 gm Sable Pastry
(see recipe page 163)

300 gm Valhrona Chocolate
(or similar dark chocolate)

100 ml Milk

175 ml Cream

2 large Eggs

CITRUS SALAD

1 Orange

1 Ruby Grapefruit

1 Mandarin

1 Tangelo

GARNISH

180 ml Double Cream

100 ml Stock Syrup
(see recipe page 162)

1 Orange (juice only)

METHOD

- Roll out sable pastry to 1/2 cm thickness and carefully line buttered, 20 cm tart tin. Rest pastry for 15 mins.
- Prick pastry with a fork and bake blind in a 180°C pre-heated oven until lightly browned (15 to 20 mins).
- Remove shell from oven and cool. Melt chocolate in a double boiler and remove from heat.
- Combine milk and cream in a medium pot and bring to the boil. Whisk eggs in a large bowl, then slowly whisk in cream and milk mixture.
- Add melted chocolate and mix well.
- Pour mix into tart shell, place tart in 180°C oven and turn oven off.
- Remove after 45 mins and allow to cool before serving.
- Peel and segment citrus fruits removing all pith and seeds.
- Strain orange juice, combine with stock syrup and bring to the boil in a small saucepan.
- Reduce to a light caramel, remove from heat and allow to cool.
- Slice tart carefully and place a slice in the centre of each plate. Divide peeled citrus segments evenly between six plates, placing citrus on one side of tart and a quenelle of double cream on the other. Drizzle plate with citrus caramel and serve.

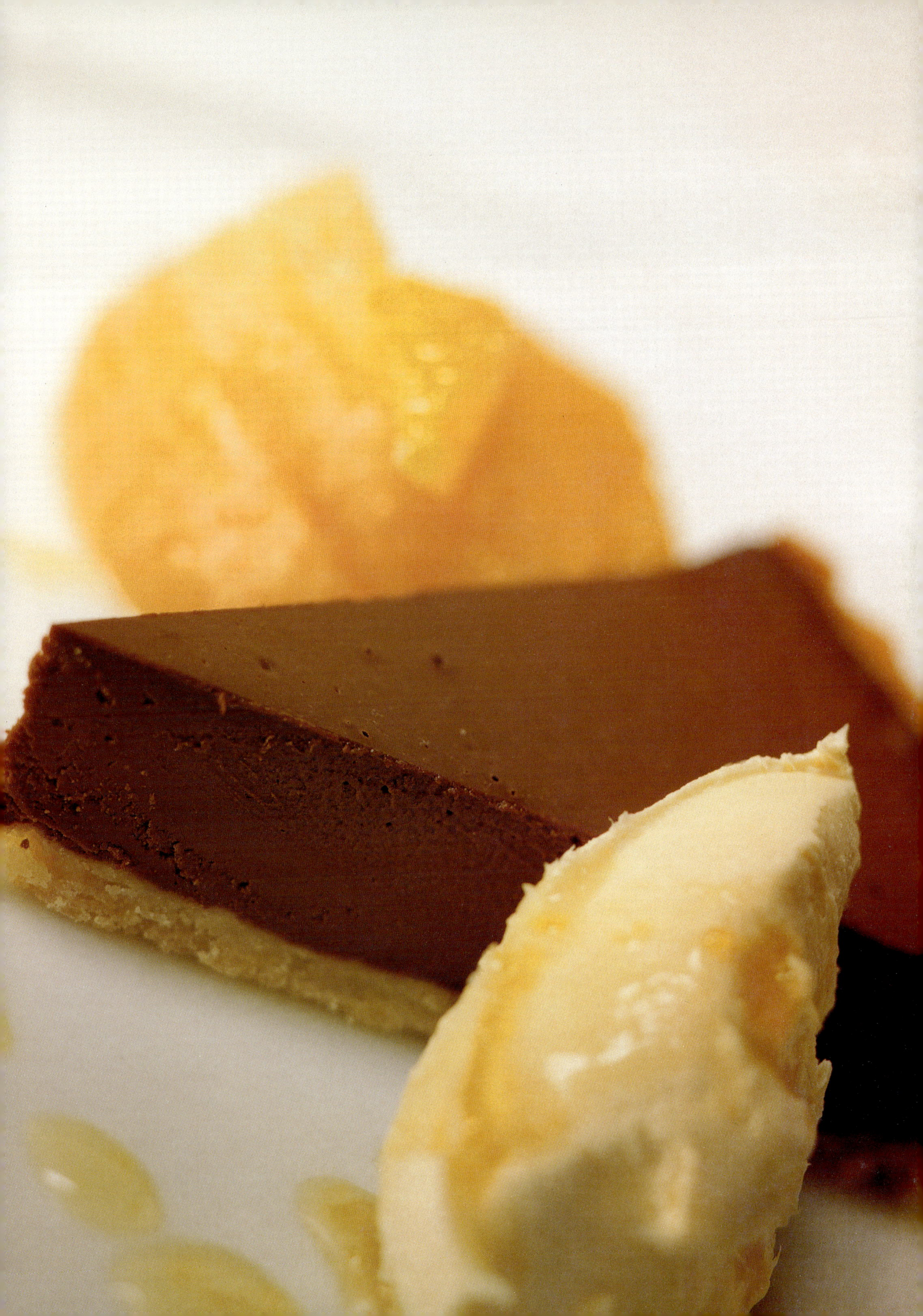

CHOCOLATE BROWNIE WITH ROAST COCONUT ICE CREAM

INGREDIENTS

180 gm Unsalted Butter

330 gm Dark Chocolate

3 Eggs

270 gm Castor Sugar

90 gm Plain Flour

360 gm Walnuts or Pecans (chopped)

Roast Coconut Ice Cream (see recipe page 161)

25 gm Coconut (shredded)

25 gm Coconut (flaked)

CHOCOLATE SAUCE

100 ml Cream

75 gm Chocolate (finely chopped)

METHOD

- Melt butter and chocolate in a double boiler.
- Beat eggs and sugar in a mixing bowl until a light creamy texture.
- Add butter and chocolate. Fold in flour and nuts then pour into a well-greased biscuit tray.
- Bake in a 180°C pre-heated oven for 20 to 25min. Remove brownie from oven and rest for 1/2 hr.
- Turn brownie out on to cake rack and rest until room temperature.
- Roast coconut in oven until lightly coloured (keep shredded and flaked separate for garnishing).
- Bring cream to the boil in a small pot, remove from heat, add chocolate and stir until dissolved.
- Slice brownie, place in the centre of plate.
- Roll coconut ice cream in shredded coconut and rest on top of brownie.
- Garnish with flaked coconut, drizzle chocolate sauce over plate and serve.

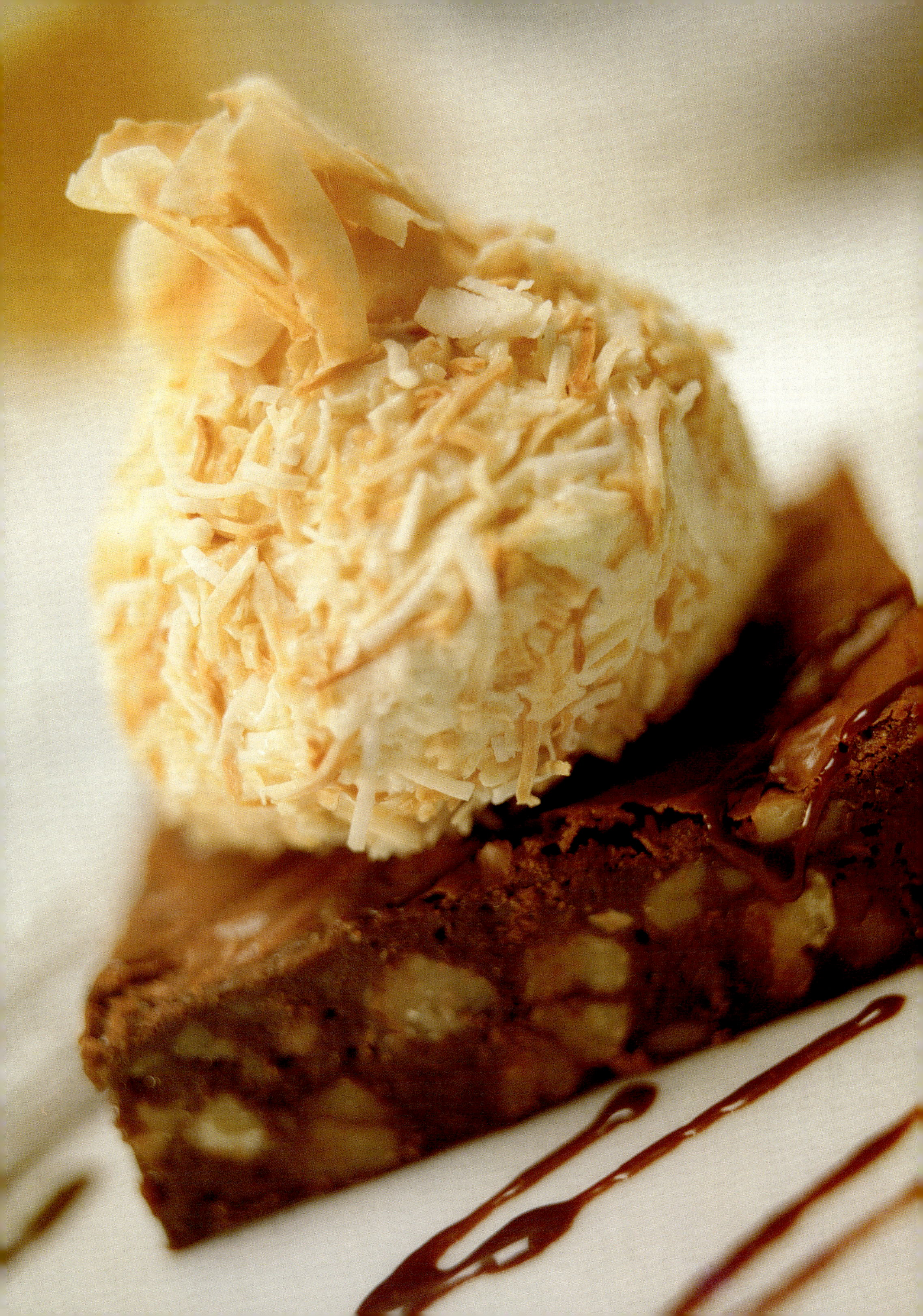

APPLE & BANANA STACK

INGREDIENTS

3 Granny Smith Apples
(peeled and cored)

3 Cavendish Bananas (ripe)

Sable Pastry
(see recipe page 163)

100 gm Unsalted Butter

50 ml Vegetable Oil

100 ml Double Cream

Banana Ice Cream
(see recipe page 160)

CARAMEL SAUCE

100 gm Unsalted Butter

100 gm Brown Sugar

200 ml Cream

METHOD

- Roll out sable pastry to 1/2 cm thickness and cut into 5 cm rounds. Rest for 20 mins and prick with a fork. Bake for 15 mins in a 180°C pre-heated oven, remove from oven and cool.
- Combine all ingredients for caramel sauce in a heavy based pot.
- Bring to the boil, allow to cool and store in a warm place.
- Peel bananas, halve lengthways and cut into quarters. Cut apples vertically into twelfths.
- Heat half butter and oil in a heavy based pan on medium heat.
- Saute apple until golden brown, remove from heat and drain on kitchen paper.
- Heat remaining butter and oil in a heavy based pan on medium heat.
- Saute bananas until flesh starts to soften, remove from heat and drain on kitchen paper.
- Rest one sable biscuit in the centre of each plate and arrange 2 pieces of banana and apple on biscuit.
- Place 1 dspn of double cream in the centre of each stack and gently press second sable biscuit onto stack.
- Layer remaining banana and apple, garnish with ice cream, liberally pour caramel sauce over and serve.

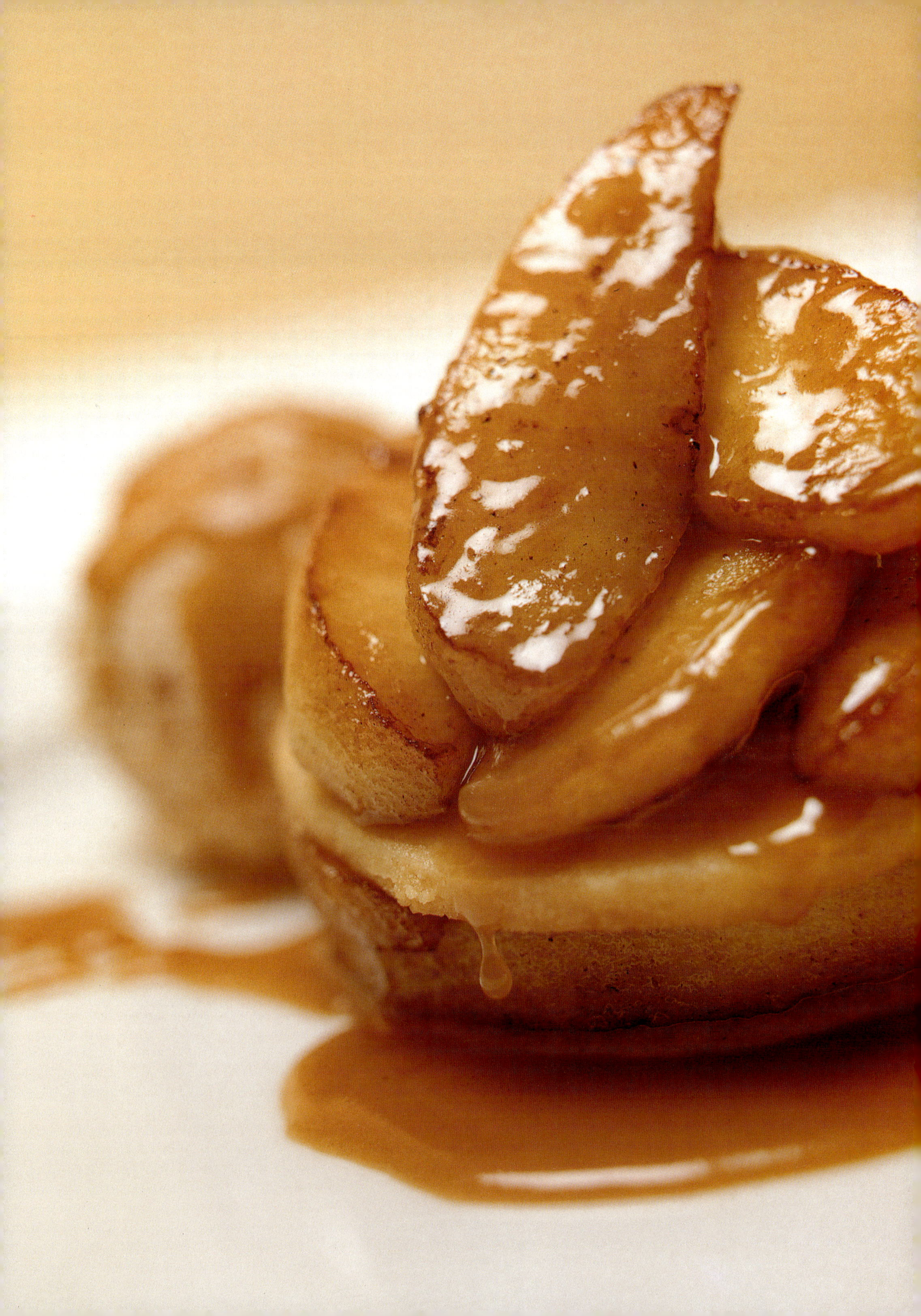

BREAD & BUTTER CUSTARD

INGREDIENTS

3 x 15 mm thick slices Sultana Bread (crusts removed)

150 ml Milk

150 ml Cream

5 large Eggs

125 gm Castor Sugar

1 Vanilla Bean

30 gm Unsalted Butter (soft)

METHOD

- Butter sultana bread and terrine mould, then lay bread into terrine mould.
- Bring milk, cream and vanilla bean to the boil in a heavy based pot, remove from heat and cool.
- Remove vanilla bean, split and scrape seeds into milk mixture.
- Whisk sugar and eggs well in a medium bowl and pour in milk mixture whisking well. Pour mix over bread and rest for 10 mins (bread must rise to surface before cooking).
- Pre-heat oven to 200°C and bring 1 litre water to the boil.
- Pour water into a small baking tray and gently rest terrine mould in water. Cook for 30 mins or until a wooden skewer can be inserted and removed cleanly.
- Remove from oven and bain-marie, cool for 10 mins.
- Cut pudding into portions and remove using a wide spatula, dust with icing sugar and serve.

NOTE

Panettone or croissants make an interesting change to this classical dish. This pudding stands well on its own, but can also be served with caramel sauce, creme anglaise or ice cream.

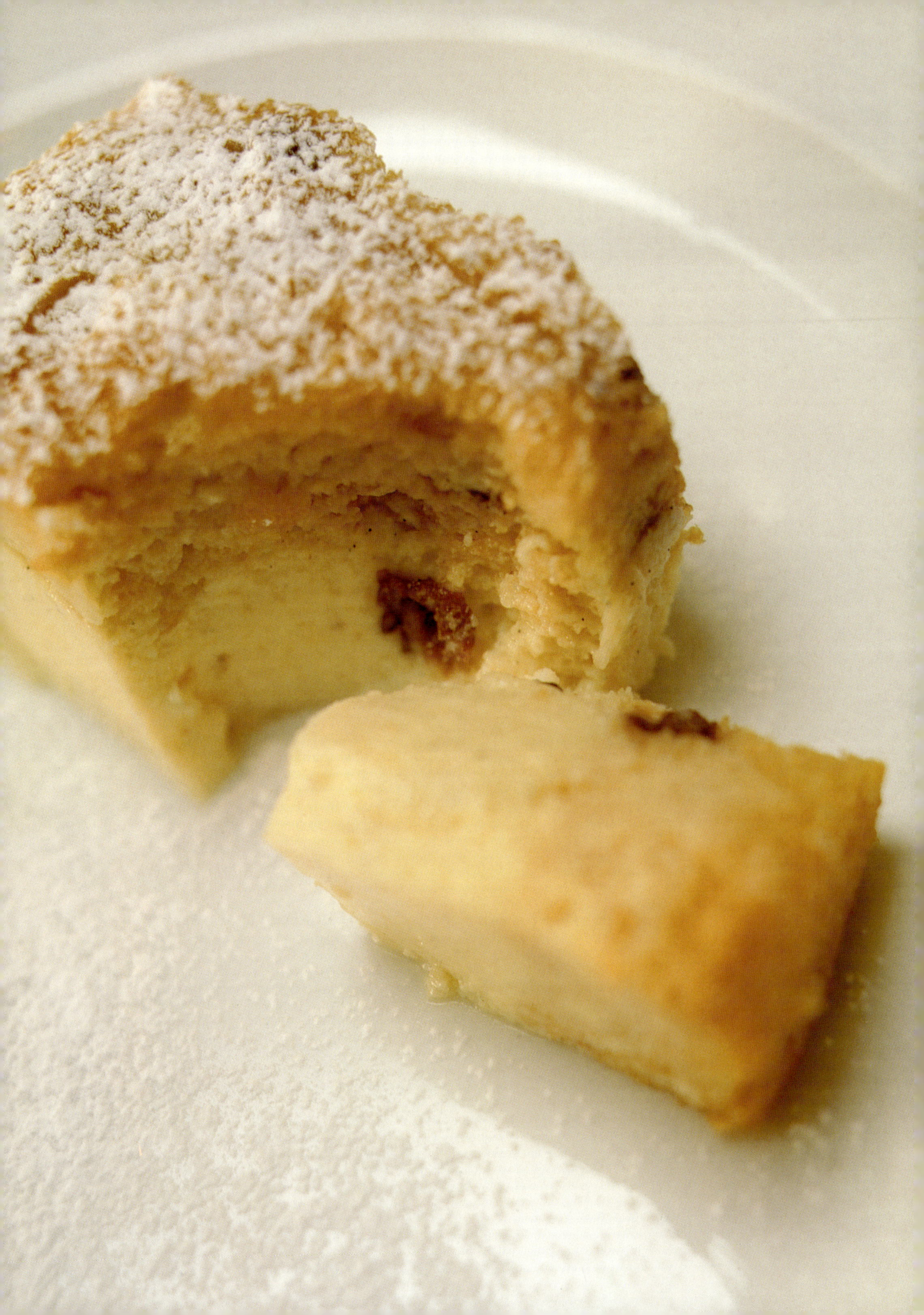

DRUNKEN FRUIT STEAMED PUDDING

INGREDIENTS

170 gm Self-raising Flour

50 gm Almond Meal

1 teasp Baking Powder

1/2 tblsp Cinnamon (ground)

1 tblsp Mixed Spice

125 gm Castor Sugar

90 gm Unsalted Butter

2 large Eggs

200 ml Milk

400 gm Drunken Fruit
(see recipe page 163)

300 ml Creme Anglaise
(see recipe page 162)

METHOD

- Separate egg yolks and whites, whip egg whites to soft peak consistency.
- Cream butter and sugar, then slowly add egg yolks.
- Add self raising-flour, almond meal, baking powder, cinnamon, mixed spice, milk and 2/3 drunken fruit slowly. Fold in egg whites and spoon into buttered pudding moulds until 2/3 full.
- Cover each pudding lightly with buttered foil.
- Pre-heat oven to 180°C and bring 1.5 litres water to the boil.
- Place puddings, well separated, in a large baking tray and gently pour in boiling water. Cook for 30 mins or until a wooden skewer can be inserted and removed cleanly.
- Remove puddings from oven and bain-marie, cool for 10 mins.
- Warm remaining drunken fruit gently in a small pot. Turn puddings out of moulds and serve topped with remaining drunken fruit.

NOTE Double cream or ice cream should be served separately with this dish.

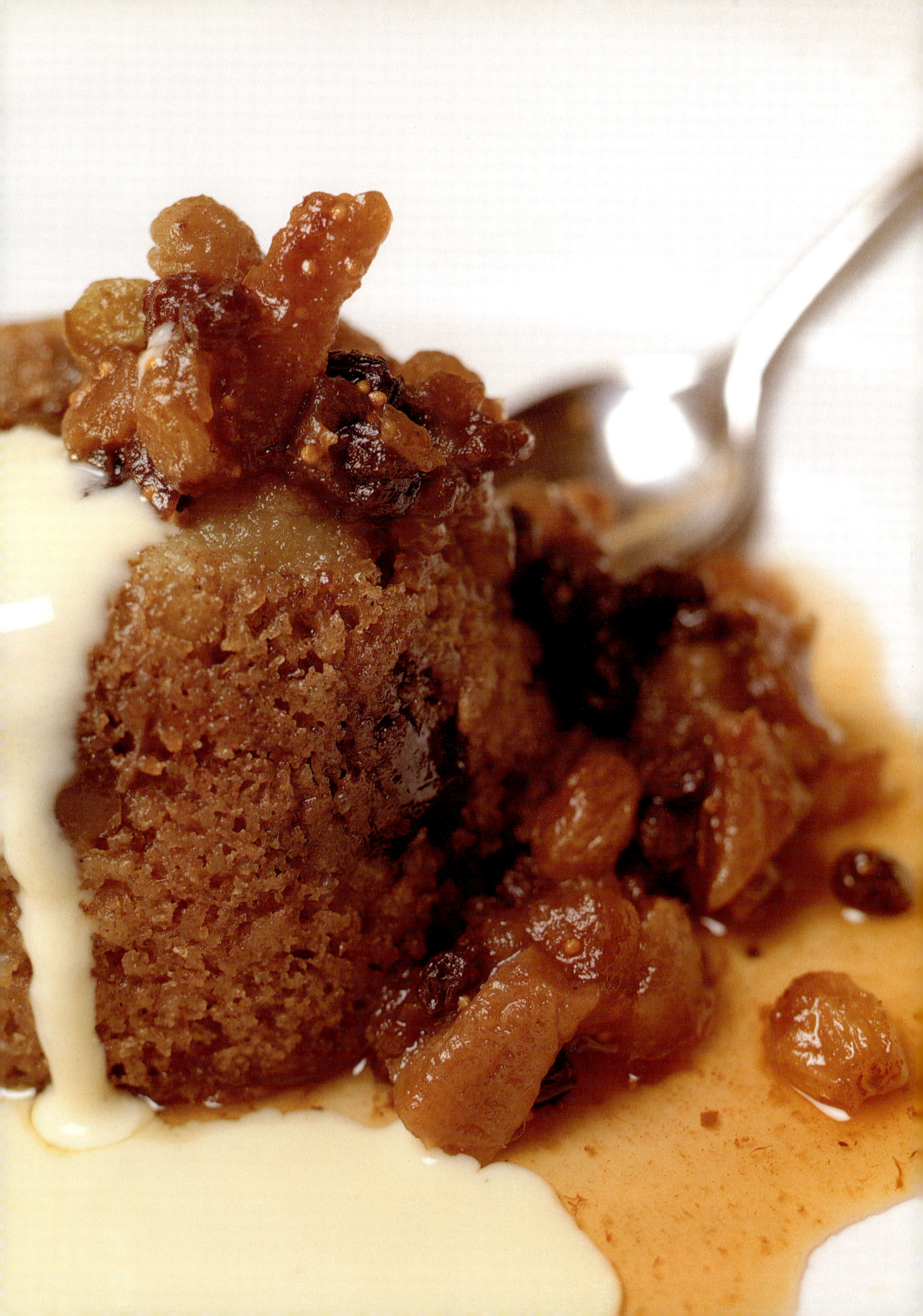

SAUTERNE CAKE & SUMMER FRUITS

INGREDIENTS

3 large Eggs	200 gm Plain Flour (sifted)
185 gm Castor Sugar	100 gm Almond Meal
1 Lemon (rind only)	2 Apricots
1 pinch Salt	2 Nectarines
12 tblsp Sauterne	2 Peaches
9 tblsp Milk	500 ml Stock Syrup (see recipe page 162)
250 ml Extra Virgin Olive Oil	
1 1/2 tblsp Baking Powder	

METHOD

- Pre-heat oven to 200°C. Beat eggs and sugar until light and creamy.
- Stir in grated lemon rind, salt, Sauterne, milk and olive oil.
- Add baking powder, almond meal and flour and mix through.
- Pour mixture into a cake tin greased with olive oil and bake for 50 mins.
- Cool for 10 mins and turn out on to a cooling rack.
- Peel, halve and remove stones from fruit. Cut each half into thirds and mix lightly in a medium bowl.
- Bring stock syrup to the boil and pour over fruit, let stand until cool.
- Cut six slices from cake and place to one side of plates. Arrange fruits beside cake and serve.

NOTE

This cake can also be served with fresh mango or citrus fruits.

HAZELNUT & ORANGE SABLE BISCUITS

INGREDIENTS 100 gm Unsalted Butter (soft)
100 gm Castor Sugar
3 large Eggs
1/4 Orange (zest only)
100 gm Plain Flour
115 gm Hazelnuts (finely chopped)

METHOD
- Combine all ingredients, except hazelnuts, in a food processor. Turn into a mixing bowl and mix in hazelnuts.
- Separate pastry into 4 pieces and rest in a cool place for 20 min. Roll each piece on a lightly floured bench until 1 cm thick.
- Cut out biscuits with a cutter and rest on a lightly-buttered baking tray for 20 min. Cook biscuits in a 180°C pre-heated oven until lightly coloured (10 to 12 min).
- Remove from oven and when cool enough to handle, rest on a cake rack until room temperature. Store in an airtight container in a cool dry place.
- Serve dusted with icing sugar.

BUTTER SHORTBREADS

INGREDIENTS 300 gm Plain Flour
200 gm Unsalted Butter
80 gm Castor Sugar
Vanilla Essence

METHOD
- Cream butter and sugar, add vanilla to taste and lastly flour (do not over work). Roll pastry into 25 mm diameter logs.
- Refrigerate until firm and slice at 8 mm intervals.
- Bake on a buttered and floured baking tray at 160°C for 15 mins or until very lightly coloured. Remove from oven and when cool enough to handle, rest on a cake rack until room temperature.
- Store in an airtight container in a cool dry place.

ALMOND ROCHERS

INGREDIENTS 200 gm Slivered Almonds   30 ml Grand Marnier
60 gm Icing Sugar   200 gm Dark Chocolate

METHOD
- Place almonds evenly in a heavy based baking tray, sprinkle with icing sugar and Grand Marnier. Toast in a moderate oven until sugar is dissolved and almonds are lightly coloured.
- Stir after removing from the oven to stop nuts from sticking together and allow to cool.
- Melt chocolate gently over a double boiler and remove from heat.
- Stir almonds into melted chocolate, spoon on to a lightly greased tray and refrigerate. When set, store in a cool dry place in an airtight container.

CHOCOLATE TRUFFLES

INGREDIENTS 500 gm Dark Chocolate   30 ml Kahlua
200 ml Cream   100 gm Cocoa Powder
10 gm Unsalted Butter

METHOD
- Heat chocolate, cream and butter gently in a double boiler (do not allow any water to contact chocolate mix) (do not allow mixture to boil).
- When combined, remove from heat, add Kahlua and allow to cool. Refrigerate mixture until firm.
- Form into small balls, roll in cocoa powder and store in a cool dry place in an airtight container.

NOTE Chocolates may also be rolled in toasted coconut or finely chopped nuts.

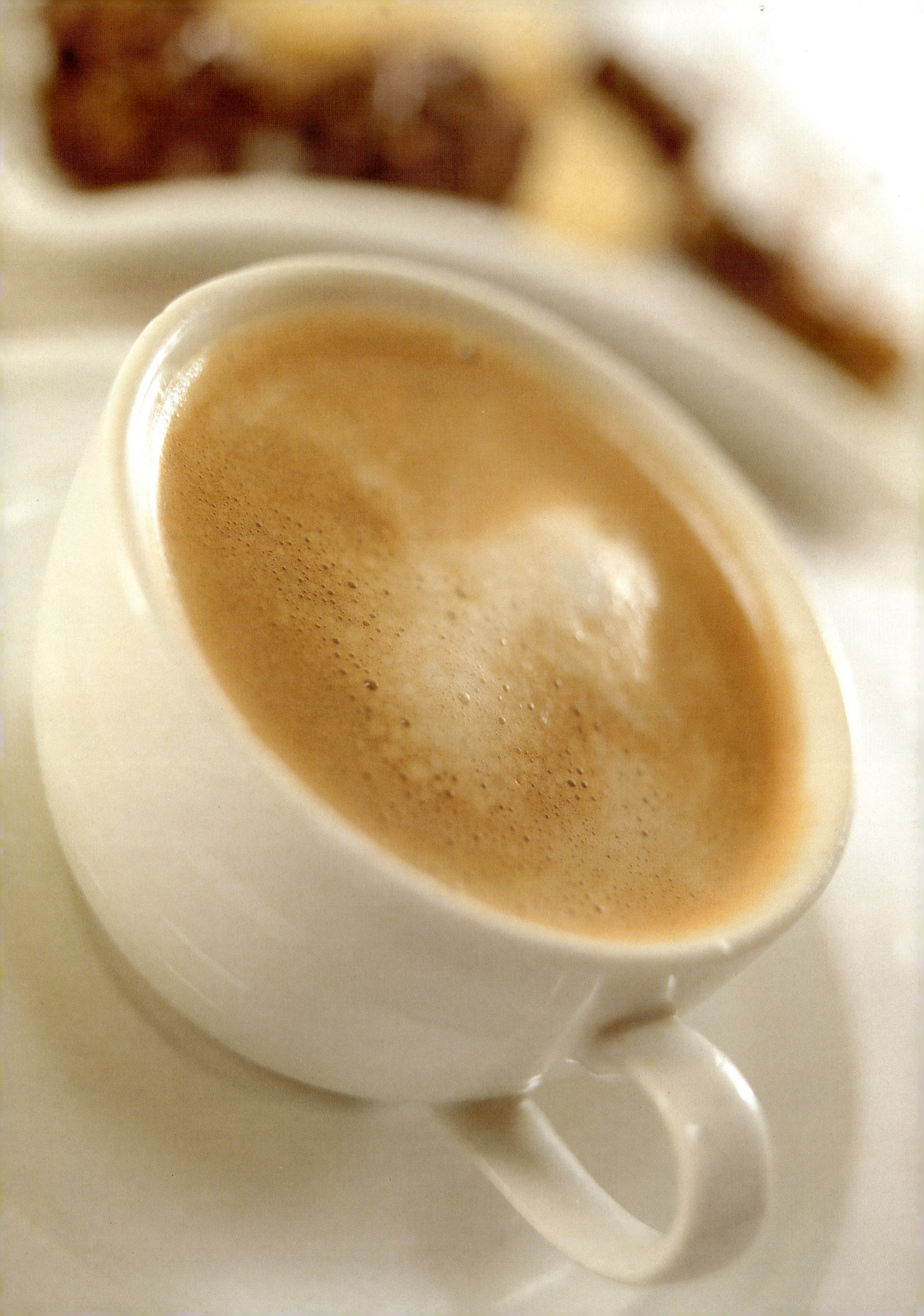

CHEESE

INGREDIENTS
Jindi Triple Cream
Milawa King River Gold
Woodside Edith Chevre
Kangaroo Island Brie
Extra Test A Reggiano
English Stilton
Royal Victorian Blue

GARNISH
Water Crackers
Oatmeal Biscuits
Wholemeal Biscuits
Green Apple
Quince Paste
Dried Muscatels

METHOD

- Compile a selection of not more than four cheeses.
- Remove any wrappings and allow cheese to stand at room temperature for at least 2 hrs before serving.
- Arrange cheese on platter without cutting into smaller pieces (whole blocks present more attractively).
- Garnish with biscuits and fruit, do not allow garnish to come into contact with cheese.

NOTE

From John MacDonald (noted Brisbane cheese providore). "Cheese is a living thing unlike many other foods you might store in the refrigerator. Whereas the life cycle of meat, fish and vegetables has ceased, cheese moves from youthful immaturity to rich, aged complexity.

When buying cheese, make your choice totally subjective and always taste before you buy! Australian specialty cheese deserves to be supported wherever possible. Our fledgling industry has come so far in such a short time. Also look for imported rarities that might emerge, the presence of classical European styles inspire the Australian cheesemaker to greater achievements.

Cheese should always be purchased in the smallest quantities for immediate, or short term consumption. The retailer is much better equipped to store the cheese, and buying frequently avoids cheese drying out or going mouldy in the home refrigerator. Care needs to be taken when storing cheese, due to its 'living' qualities cheese needs to breathe and thereby will absorb extraneous odours.

Cheese can be served at any time, but in a structured meal we have much to learn from the French who have long displayed a reverence for cheese by serving it after the main course. This ritual avoids moving from a savoury course to a sweet dessert and back again to a savoury course. In French tradition their best aged wines are served with the cheese as it enhances the finest qualities of the wine."

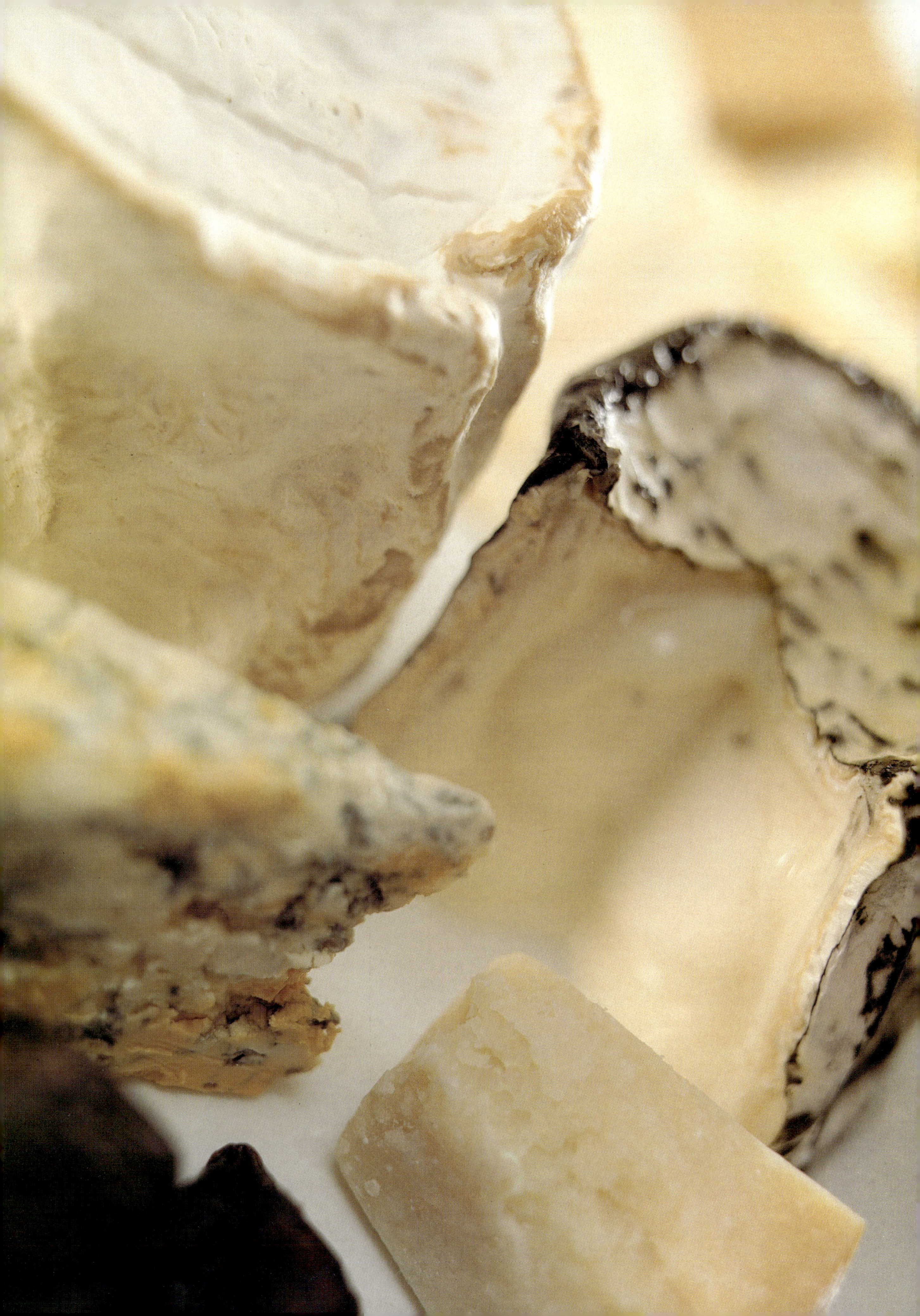

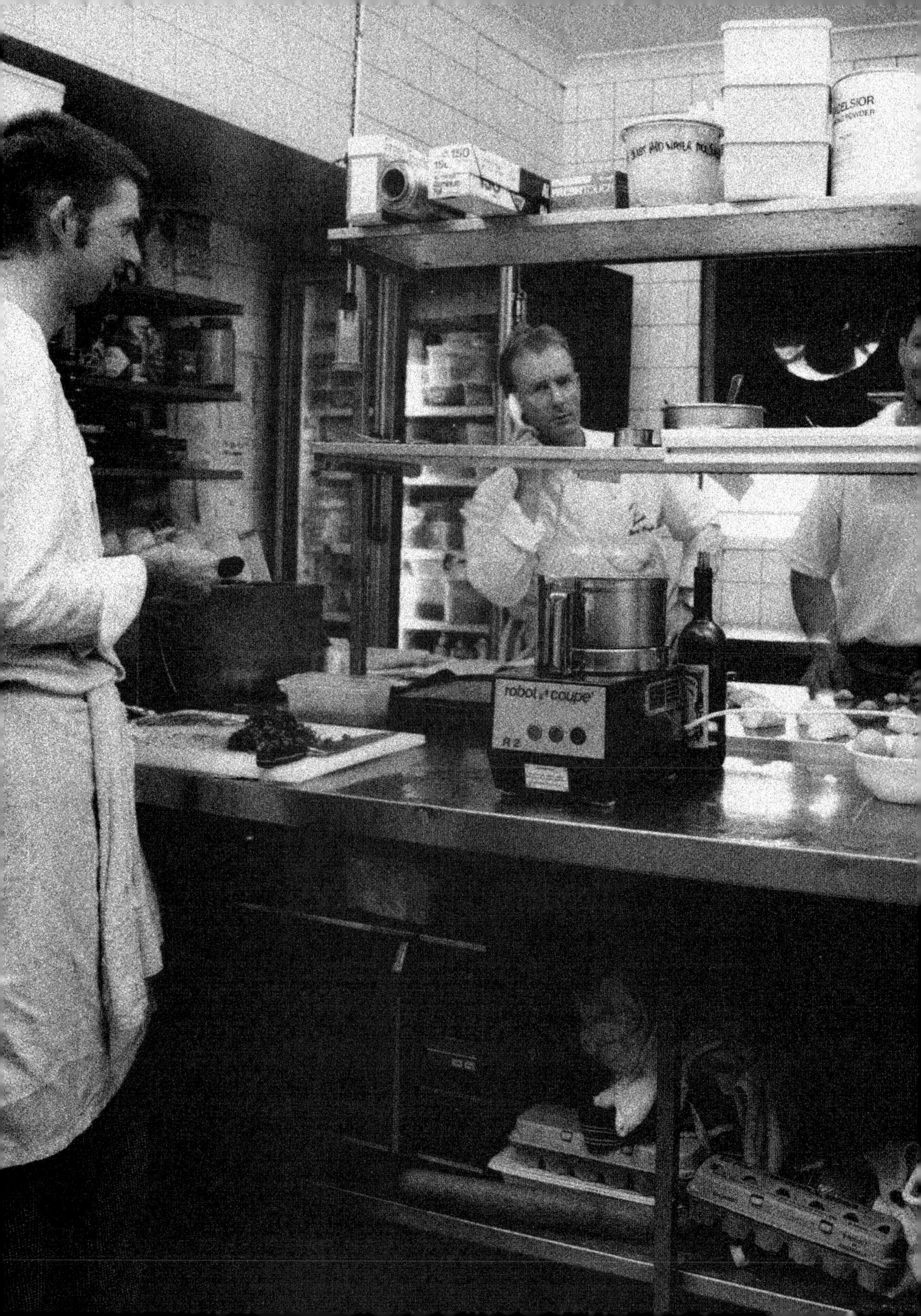
robot coupe
R 2

BASE RECIPES

Small Rooms 2

Use these recipes instead of packaged components and gain the rewards of time and patience.

STOCKS & SAUCES

VEAL STOCK

INGREDIENTS
- 2 kg Veal Bones
- 1/2 Pig's Trotter
- 1 small Carrot (peeled and roughly chopped)
- 1 Celery Stick (roughly chopped)
- 1 Brown Onion (peeled and roughly chopped)
- 1 desp Tomato Paste
- 8 cloves Garlic
- 12 Black Peppercorns
- 1/2 Bay Leaf

METHOD
- Roast bones, trotter, carrot, celery, onion and tomato paste in a 180°C oven until well coloured.
- Tip bones and vegetables into a large stock pot, add remaining ingredients. Just cover with water and bring to the boil.
- Reduce heat to simmer, remove any scum from surface and cook for 12 hrs removing scum as necessary, top up water if needed.
- Remove stock from heat and strain, cool and store in an airtight container in refrigerator.

CHICKEN STOCK

INGREDIENTS
- 1 kg Chicken Bones
- 1 medium Carrot
- 1 medium Brown Onion
- 1 Celery Stick
- 1 Leek (white part only)
- 2 sprigs Thyme
- 8 cloves Garlic
- 12 Black Peppercorns
- 2 Cloves

METHOD
- Cut carrot, onion, celery, leek and garlic roughly.
- Cover chicken bones with 3 litres water in a large pot and bring to the boil. Reduce heat and skim top to remove scum.
- Add all remaining ingredients and boil gently for 3 to 4 hrs. Keep skimming as any scum appears.
- Remove from heat, strain and cool. Place stock in refrigerator, when cold remove any fat or scum remaining on surface.
- Store in an airtight container in refrigerator.

PEKING DUCK STOCK

INGREDIENTS
- 2 litres Chicken Stock
- 1 kg Peking Duck Bones
- 1 piece Dried Mandarin Peel
- 1/2 Brown Onion (sliced)
- 1 small Carrot (chopped)
- 1/2 stick Celery (chopped)
- 6 cloves Garlic
- 10 Black Peppercorns

METHOD
- Add all ingredients to 1 litre water and bring to the boil in a stock pot.
- Reduce heat and simmer for 2 1/2 hrs.
- Pass stock through a fine strainer and cool.
- Store in an airtight container in refrigerator.

COURT BOUILLON

INGREDIENTS
- 50 ml White Wine Vinegar
- 10 gm Salt
- 1/2 small Carrot (sliced)
- 1/4 White Onion (sliced)
- 1/4 Celery Stick (sliced)
- 1 Bay Leaf
- 1 sprig Thyme
- 6 Black Peppercorns
- 2 Parsley Stalks

METHOD
- Add all ingredients to 1 litre water and bring to the boil in a stock pot.
- Reduce to simmer for 1 hr and cool.
- Strain and store in an airtight container in refrigerator.

DEMI GLACE

METHOD
- Reduce 1 litre of veal stock by 1/2.
- Store in an airtight container in refrigerator.

BEEF JUS

INGREDIENTS
1 litre Veal Demi Glace
250 ml Veal Stock
100 gm roasted Beef Trimmings
4 shallots (sliced and browned)
2 cloves Garlic
10 Black Peppercorns
1/2 Bay Leaf

METHOD
- Bring all ingredients to the boil in a heavy based pot.
- Reduce to simmer for 1 hr, pass through a fine sieve and serve or store in an airtight container in the refrigerator.

LAMB JUS

INGREDIENTS
1 litre Veal Demi Glace
250 ml Veal Stock
100 gm Roasted Lamb Bones or Trimmings
4 shallots (sliced and browned)
8 cloves Garlic
10 Black Peppercorns
1/2 Bay Leaf

METHOD
- Bring all ingredients to the boil in a heavy based pot.
- Reduce to simmer for 1 hr, pass through a fine sieve and serve or store in an airtight container in the refrigerator.

VENISON JUS

INGREDIENTS
500 ml Veal Demi Glace
100 gm Roasted Venison Trimmings
4 shallots (peeled and sliced)
2 cloves Garlic
4 Juniper Berries (crushed)
10 Black Peppercorns (crushed)

METHOD
- Bring all ingredients to the boil in a heavy based pot.
- Reduce to simmer for 1 hr, pass through a fine sieve and serve or store in an airtight container in the refrigerator.

CHICKEN JUS

INGREDIENTS

1 litre Chicken Stock
100 gm Roasted Chicken Bones
6 Shallots (sliced and browned)
1 clove Garlic
6 Black Peppercorns
1/2 Bay Leaf
5 gm Cornflour
25 ml Water

METHOD

- Bring all ingredients to the boil in a heavy based pot.
- Reduce to simmer for 1 hr, pass through a fine sieve and serve or store in an airtight container in the refrigerator.

PEKING DUCK SAUCE

INGREDIENTS

1 litre Peking Duck Stock (or Chicken Stock)
250 ml Demi Glace
100 gm Peking Duck Bones
6 Shallots (peeled and sliced)
6 Sichuan Peppercorns
1/2 Star Anise
1/2 Bay Leaf
1/2 Mandarin (juice only)
2 desp Coconut Vinegar
1 desp Sambal Oelek
2 desp Palm Sugar
1 Kaffir Lime Leaf
2 Coriander Roots
1 sprig Mint

METHOD

- Bring stock, demi glace, bones, shallots, peppercorns, star anise and bay leaf to the boil in a heavy based pot. Reduce by 1/2 then add remaining ingredients.
- Return to boil and reduce to simmer. Cook for 5 mins, pass through a fine sieve and serve.

MUSTARD SAUCE

INGREDIENTS

250 ml Chicken Stock
6 Shallots (sliced)
500 ml Cream
1 tblsp Seeded Mustard
50 gm Butter
ground Black Pepper

METHOD

- Reduce cream, shallots and chicken stock by 1/2. Whisk in mustard and butter. Season to taste with black pepper and serve.

MADEIRA SAUCE

INGREDIENTS 250 ml Madeira
200 gm Beef Trimmings
1 litre Demi Glace
250 ml Veal Stock
4 Shallots (peeled and sliced)
1 clove Garlic
1/2 Bay Leaf

METHOD
- Bring Madeira to the boil in a heavy based pot and reduce by 3/4.
- Add remaining ingredients and return to the boil. Reduce to simmer for 1 hr. Season with salt and pepper, pass through a fine sieve and serve or store in an airtight container.

BORDELAISE SAUCE

INGREDIENTS 250 ml Demi Glace
500 ml Red Wine
20 Shallots (peeled and sliced)
50 gm Butter
50 gm Bone Marrow (chopped)

METHOD
- In a heavy based pot bring red wine and shallots to the boil and reduce by 2/3.
- Add demi glace, return to boil and whisk in butter and marrow. Strain through a fine sieve and serve immediately. Sauce cannot be stored.

NOTE Reduction and demi glace can be prepared in advance, but do not add butter or marrow until serving.

FOIE GRAS BUTTER

INGREDIENTS 250 ml Chicken Stock
350 ml Cream
100 gm Butter (soft)
150 gm Foie Gras Pate

METHOD
- Bring chicken stock and cream to the boil in a heavy based pot and reduce by 1/2. Allow to cool for 10 mins then whisk in butter and pate.
- Season to taste with salt and pepper, strain and serve.

NOTE Reduction and demi glace can be prepared in advance, but do not add butter or foie gras until serving.

DRESSINGS

BASE MAYONNAISE

INGREDIENTS
- 2 Egg Yolks
- 2 teasp Dijon Mustard
- 600 ml Vegetable Oil
- 4 teasp White Wine Vinegar
- 1 Lemon (juice only)

METHOD
- Mix egg yolks and mustard in a food processor, very slowly add oil to make mayonnaise.
- Finish with vinegar and lemon juice and refrigerate.

AIOLI

INGREDIENTS
- 2 tblsp White Wine Vinegar
- 250 ml Olive Oil
- 1 teasp Dijon Mustard
- 8 cloves Roasted Garlic
- 1 Egg Yolk
- juice 1/4 Lemon

METHOD
- Puree vinegar, mustard, roast garlic, egg yolk and lemon juice in a food processor. Add oil slowly until emulsified.

HERB OIL

INGREDIENTS
- 1 cup Basil Leaves
- 1 cup Parsley Leaves
- 1 tblsp Thyme Leaves
- 200 ml Vegetable Oil
- 100 ml Olive Oil

METHOD
- Blend all ingredients in a food processor on high for 1 min.
- Strain into a bottle and store in refrigerator.

YELLOW CURRY OIL

INGREDIENTS

- 500 ml Vegetable Oil
- 3 Cardamom Pods
- 1/2 tblsp Coriander Seed
- 1/4 tblsp Cumin Seed
- 1/4 tblsp whole Black Peppercorns
- 1/4 small knob Ginger (roughly chopped)
- 1/4 Cinnamon Quill
- 3 Cloves
- pinch grated Nutmeg
- 1/2 head Garlic
- 1/4 tblsp Fenugreek
- 1 Bay Leaf
- 2 Kaffir Lime Leaves
- 1 tblsp Turmeric
- 1 teasp Garam Masala

METHOD

- Warm all ingredients (except lime leaves, garlic and vegetable oil) in a heavy based pan on low heat for 5 mins. Remove from heat and cool.
- Combine all ingredients in a food processor, stand in a cool place overnight, strain and store in refrigerator.

YELLOW CURRY PASTE

INGREDIENTS

- 6 Shallots (sliced)
- 6 cloves Garlic
- 1 teasp ground White Pepper
- 1 teasp Salt
- 1 teasp Garam Masala
- 2 desp Turmeric
- 1 stem Lemongrass (roughly chopped)
- 1 teasp Cumin (ground)
- 4 Cardamom Pods
- 2 Coriander Roots (roughly chopped)
- 4 Kaffir Lime Leaves
- 2 teasp Sambal Oelek
- 1/2 cup Water

METHOD

- Combine all ingredients in a food processor and blend to a smooth paste.

NAM PRIK SAUCE

INGREDIENTS   4 tblsp Nam Prik   3 Limes
                  2 teasp Sambal Oelek   6 cloves Garlic (peeled)
                  100 ml Ketchap Manis   5 Coriander Roots
                  500 gm Palm Sugar   1 tablsp Chopped Mint

METHOD
- Juice limes and puree garlic in juice.
- Add all other ingredients and blend well.
- Add water to make a smooth sauce like consistency. Pass through a fine strainer. Store in sterile jars in refrigerator

GARNISHES

PUFF PASTRY

INGREDIENTS   750 gm Plain Flour   25 gm Salt
                  600 gm Butter   350 ml Iced Water

METHOD
- Work 100 gm butter, salt and flour together until mixture resembles breadcrumbs. Add water and knead to form a smooth dough. Rest paste for 20 mins.
- Roll out dough to a large rectangle (approx. 2 cm thick) on a floured board.
- Spread remaining butter roughly over half the area, fold remaining dough over and ensure edges are sealed.
- Fold dough in half, turn dough in opposite direction and roll out quickly. Use plenty of flour so butter does not break through dough.
- Fold in half once again, rest for one hour and repeat roll and fold process. Repeat three more times.

PARMESAN BRIOCHE

INGREDIENTS
- 1 1/2 cups Plain Flour
- 1/2 teasp Salt
- 1 desp Sugar
- 1 tblsp Tepid Water
- 15 gm Yeast (fresh)
- 3 large Eggs
- 1 Egg Yolk
- 100 gm Parmesan Cheese (grated)
- 160 gm Unsalted Butter (room temp)

METHOD
- Sift flour and salt. Dissolve sugar in tepid water in a large mixing bowl and add yeast, stirring slowly until dissolved.
- Add flour, salt, eggs and yolk, mix until smooth.
- Add 3/4 of parmesan cheese, then gradually add butter mixing well.
- Cover bowl with cling wrap and leave to prove in a warm place until mix has doubled in size.
- Turn mix out of bowl on to a floured bench.
- Cut dough to desired size for moulds (note that dough will double in size when cooked).
- Place dough in well buttered moulds and allow to prove until doubled in size again.
- Pre-heat oven to 200°C.
- Brush loaves with egg wash, sprinkle with remaining parmesan and bake in oven for 20 mins or until loaves are rich golden brown.
- Remove from oven, cool for 10 mins and turn out of moulds on to a cake rack.
- Loaves should be wrapped well in cling wrap and stored in freezer in an airtight container if brioche is not being used straight away.

SPAETZLI

INGREDIENTS
- 2 Large Eggs
- 250 gm Plain Flour (sifted)
- 50 ml Milk
- 1 desp Olive Oil

METHOD
- Combine all ingredients in a food processor until a smooth paste (like thick beer batter), allow to rest for 30 mins.
- Bring 1.5 litres salted water to the boil. Press paste through a colander allowing pieces approx. 3 cm long to fall into boiling water.
- Return to boil and cook for 1 min, drain and dry on kitchen paper.

POTATO MASH

INGREDIENTS 4 medium sized Potatoes (peeled and sliced)

50 ml Cream

75 gm Butter

METHOD
- Boil potatoes for 15 mins (or until soft), drain away water and pass through a mouli and or blend in a food processor.
- Beat in butter and cream, season with salt and pepper then serve.

SOFT POLENTA

INGREDIENTS 250 gm Polenta

600 ml Milk

600 ml Chicken Stock

1/2 Bay Leaf

1 sprig Thyme

1 Basil Leaf

50 ml Olive Oil

150 gm Parmesan (grated)

100 gm Unsalted Butter

METHOD
- Bring milk, stock, herbs and oil to the boil in a heavy based pot.
- Reduce to simmer and remove herbs, add polenta slowly, stirring constantly.
- Reduce to low heat and cook for 20 mins stirring constantly.
- Stir in parmesan and butter, season to taste with salt and pepper and serve.

POACHED EGGS

INGREDIENTS 2 litres Water

1/4 cup White Vinegar

2 desp Salt

6 Eggs

METHOD
- Bring water, vinegar and salt to a gentle boil in a deep pan.
- Add eggs gently by pouring out of a coffee cup or wide-mouthed sauce-boat.
- Cook for 2 mins and remove gently with slotted spoon. Trim off rough edges and serve.

ONION CONFIT

INGREDIENTS 1/4 cup Olive Oil 55 gm Castor Sugar

1 kg Brown Onions 1/4 cup White Wine Vinegar
(peeled and sliced)

METHOD
- Heat oil in a heavy based pan, add onions and cook on high heat until coloured, reduce heat, stir in sugar and vinegar, leave on low heat and stir occasionally.
- Add vinegar and stir well until onion caramelises, remove from heat and season to taste.

CAPSICUM JAM

INGREDIENTS 8 Red Capsicums 150 gm Brown Sugar

1 large Salad Onion 150 ml Red Wine Vinegar
(peeled and sliced)

METHOD
- Roast red capsicums in a hot oven until skin is blistered and well coloured. Cool, remove skin and seeds.
- Place capsicum, vinegar and chopped onion into a large pot and cover with brown sugar. Cook on moderate heat, stirring frequently until caramelised and almost toffee like.
- Take off heat and cool, puree and store in refrigerator in an airtight container.

LEEK MOUSSELINE

INGREDIENTS 100 gm Leeks (peeled and chopped) 1 large Egg

60 ml Cream 15 gm Butter

METHOD
- Cook leeks in salted boiling water for 10 mins, drain and allow to cool.
- Combine leeks, cream and egg in a food processor and blend until smooth.
- Spoon mix into six well-buttered ramekins. Cook in a bain-marie in 180°C oven for 20 mins.

ROAST GARLIC

INGREDIENTS 20 large cloves Garlic
2 sprigs Thyme
1 desp Maldon Salt
2 Bay Leaves
1 tblsp Olive Oil

METHOD
- Wrap all ingredients together well in a foil parcel. Roast on a tray in 180°C oven for 40 mins. When parcel has cooled, drain oil from garlic.

ROAST SHALLOTS

INGREDIENTS 20 Shallots
1 tblsp Olive Oil
1 desp Maldon Salt

METHOD
- Sprinkle oil and salt over shallots in a small oven dish. Roast in 180°C oven for 20 mins and serve.

ICE CREAM

VANILLA BEAN ICE CREAM

INGREDIENTS 6 Egg Yolks   600 ml Cream

160 gm Castor Sugar   2 Vanilla Beans

METHOD
- Heat vanilla beans and cream (do not boil).
- Cream egg yolks and sugar then slowly add vanilla cream mix.
- Heat in bain-marie until mix lightly coats the back of a wooden spoon.
- Remove from heat and allow to cool. Remove vanilla beans, split and scrape seeds into mix.
- Freeze mix in an ice cream maker or a round bowl, whisking rapidly every 5 mins until set.

BANANA ICE CREAM

METHOD
- Puree 2 cavendish bananas and juice of one lemon.
- Add puree to vanilla ice cream base before freezing.

BLACK SAMBUCCA ICE CREAM

INGREDIENTS 750 ml Vanilla Ice Cream Base   90 ml Black Sambucca

6 Star Anise

METHOD
- Add star anise to vanilla ice cream base when vanilla bean is added.
- Remove star anise with vanilla beans, split vanilla bean and scrape seeds into mix. When mix starts to set add liqueur and freeze as for vanilla ice cream.

LEMON MYRTLE ICE CREAM

METHOD
- Add 10 lemon myrtle leaves to vanilla ice cream base when vanilla bean is added. Store custard overnight before straining and freezing.

ROAST COCONUT ICE CREAM

METHOD
- Substitute 100 ml coconut cream for 100 ml cream in vanilla ice cream and add 30 gm roasted desicated coconut to mix as it starts to freeze.

WHITE CHOCOLATE ICE CREAM

METHOD
- Make vanilla ice cream base and stir in 350 gm grated white chocolate while mix is still warm.

RED WINE ICE CREAM

INGREDIENTS
750 ml Red Wine
50 ml Liquid Glucose
130 gm Castor Sugar
600 ml Cream
6 Egg Yolks
1 Vanilla Bean

METHOD
- Reduce red wine until 100 ml remains then add glucose.
- Heat vanilla bean and cream (do not boil).
- Cream egg yolks and sugar then slowly add vanilla cream mix.
- Heat in bain-marie until mix lightly coats the back of a wooden spoon.
- Remove from heat, add red wine syrup and allow to cool.
- Freeze mix in an ice cream maker or a round bowl stirring well every 10 mins.

DESSERT BASES

STOCK SYRUP

INGREDIENTS 500 gm Castor Sugar

1 Vanilla Bean

METHOD
- Bring 500 ml water, sugar and vanilla bean to the boil for 5 mins.
- Remove from heat and when cool, store in refrigerator in a sealed container.

CREME ANGLAISE

INGREDIENTS 200 ml Cream   60 gm Castor Sugar

2 Egg Yolks   1 Vanilla Bean

METHOD
- Heat vanilla bean and cream (do not boil).
- Cream egg yolks and sugar then slowly add vanilla cream mix.
- Heat in bain-marie until mix lightly coats the back of a wooden spoon.
- Remove from heat and allow to cool. Remove vanilla bean from mix before serving.

RASPBERRY PUREE

INGREDIENTS 300 gm frozen Raspberries

100 ml Stock Syrup

METHOD
- De-frost raspberries and mix in a food processor with syrup.
- Pass through a fine sieve and refrigerate.

CANDIED ZEST

INGREDIENTS 2 Oranges   300 gm Castor Sugar
(zest only in long thin pieces)
extra Castor Sugar
2 Lemons
(zest only in long thin pieces)

METHOD
- Blanch zest in boiling water for 2 mins and drain.
- Dissolve 300 gm castor sugar in 150 ml boiling water.
- Add zest, reduce to simmer and cook for 30 mins (zest should be translucent and tender).
- Remove from liquid and cool zest on a cake rack and store packed in castor sugar in an air tight container.

DRUNKEN FRUIT

INGREDIENTS
- 150 gm dried Figs (roughly chopped)
- 80 gm Prunes (roughly chopped)
- 80 gm dried Currants
- 80 gm Sultanas
- 80 gm Raisins
- 40 gm Mixed Peel
- 1 Cinnamon Quill
- 1 litre Stock Syrup
- 50 ml Rum
- 50 ml Brandy

METHOD
- Bring stock syrup and cinnamon quill to the boil in a medium pot.
- Add dried fruit and reduce to low heat for 10 mins.
- Remove from heat, add alcohol and allow to cool.
- Store in airtight container in refrigerator for 1 month before using.

SABLE PASTRY

INGREDIENTS
- 200 gm Unsalted Butter (room temperature)
- 75 gm Icing Sugar
- 250 gm Plain Flour
- 1/4 teasp Vanilla Essence

METHOD
- Cream butter and sugar, add vanilla and slowly work in flour.
- Wrap tightly in cling wrap and rest in a cool place for 1 hr.

TUILE

INGREDIENTS
- 500 gm Sugar
- 250 gm Egg White
- 250 gm Flour
- 250 gm Butter (melted)

METHOD
- Combine 1/2 sugar with egg white and beat to soft peak consistency.
- Combine butter and remaining sugar in a separate bowl.
- Gently add egg whites to butter mix.
- Fold in flour to make a thick gluey paste.
- Spread in a thin layer on a greased and floured oven tray and bake in a moderate oven until lightly coloured (approx. 5 mins).
- Cut into desired shape while hot, remove from tray with spatula and allow to cool on a flat surface.
- When cool store in an airtight container and use within three days.
- Unused mixture can be stored in refrigerator for one week.

GLOSSARY

ARBORIO RICE - short grained, very absorbent rice from northern Italy.

ANGLAISE - see CREME ANGLAISE

AIOLI - garlic flavoured mayonnaise.

ARMAGNAC - distilled brandy spirit from France.

ASIAN VERMICELLI NOODLES - very fine rice or bean paste noodles, can be served hot or cold, available from Asian supermarkets.

BAIN-MARIE - dish filled with water and used to cook at even temperatures, often for baking custards and puddings.

BAKE BLIND - to cook empty pastry shell for tarts and pies. Usually weighted down with grains separated from pastry by baking paper.

BALSAMIC VINEGAR - sweet, aged, wine vinegar from Modena, Italy.

BEARNAISE SAUCE - a rich, emulsified, herb-butter sauce.

BEURRE BLANC - literally white butter, made with reduction of wine, shallots and butter.

BINTJE - waxy potato best suited for mash or chips.

BLACK FUNGUS - Asian vegetable usually found dried in Asian supermarkets, expands dramatically when soaked in water overnight.

BLACK TRUFFLE - subterranean fungus with intense aroma that adds depth and richness to dishes.

BLACK TRUFFLE OIL - oil infused with black truffle, used in dressings and sauces.

BLANCH - to cook lightly in boiling water.

BORDELAISE - rich, veal stock, reduction sauce finished with bone marrow and butter.

BORLOTTI BEANS - rich, meaty flavoured bean used in Mediterranean cooking.

BRAISAGE - liquid and sauce used in braising.

BRAISE - To cook slowly in a flavoured sauce

BROTH - un-thickened stock based soup.

BRUSCHETTA - Italian bread toasted or char-grilled with olive oil and garlic.

CARDAMOM - fragrant spice used in curries and sweets from Asian and Mediterranean regions.

CARAWAY - fragrant spice with light aniseed flavour used in European cooking.

CHERMOULAH - spicy marinade used in Moroccan cooking.

CHERVIL - delicately flavoured member of the parsley family.

CHEVRE - Goat's cheese, sometimes aged in vine ash. Stands well on its own or served in salads.

CHOY SUM - crisp, green Asian vegetable available from greengrocers and Asian supermarkets.

COCONUT VINEGAR - sweet vinegar available from Asian supermarkets.

CONFIT - vegetable or meat cooked in fat (preferably goose) until soft.

CONSOMME - light, clear broth served as an appetiser or between courses.

COS (Romaine) - very crisp, lightly flavoured lettuce used in salads.

COURT BOUILLON - fragrant, spiced liquid used for poaching.

COUS COUS - cracked wheat cereal used in Middle Eastern cooking.

CREME ANGLAISE - very light vanilla custard.

CREME BRULEE (burnt cream) - a rich custard usually served with a burnt sugar crust.

CUMIN - aromatic and slightly peppery spice used in Asian and Middle Eastern cooking.

CUTTLEFISH - firm-fleshed seafood of the same family as squid.

DAIKON - very large white radish with a mild flavour available from greengrocers and Asian supermarkets.

DEMI GLACE - reduced veal stock used as a base for sauces.

DOUBLE BOILER - bowl rested over a saucepan of hot or boiling water, often used for melting chocolate or cooking Bearnaise sauce.

DOUBLE CREAM - richly flavoured cream with high fat content.

FENNEL BULB - aniseed flavoured vegetable used in European cooking.

FISH SAUCE - light brown, salty sauce used in Southern Asian cooking.

FOIE GRAS - livers or pate from force fed poultry.

GALANGAL GINGER - very aromatic ginger used in South-East Asian cooking.

GARAM MASALA - blend of fragrant curry spices.

GNOCCHI - Mediterranean pasta dumplings.

GOATS CHEESE - see CHEVRE.

GUINEA FOWL - richly flavoured, white fleshed, game bird, can be ordered from good butchers and poultry shops.

HOI SIN SAUCE - sweet barbecue sauce made from soy beans and garlic.

JAPANESE EGGPLANT - lightly flavoured, small, zucchini shaped vegetable.

JASMINE RICE - fragrant, long-grain rice.

JULIENNE - to cut a vegetable very finely (about the size of a match stick).

JUNIPER BERRIES - rich and aromatic spice, mainly used with game.

JUS - un-thickened reduction sauce.

KAFFIR LIME LEAVES - highly aromatic spice used in South-East Asian cooking.

KETCHAP MANIS - sweet and intense soy sauce from Indonesia.

KIPFLER - small, elongated, waxy potato.

LEMON MYRTLE - native spice with a fragrant, lemon flavour.

LINGUINE - thin, flat pasta.

MADEIRA - fortified wine not dissimilar to but drier than port.

MALDON SEA SALT - large, brittle salt crystals with intense flavour.

MASCARPONE - a soft, creamy cheese used in Italian desserts.

MESCLUN SALAD MIX - blend of lettuce leaves readily available from greengrocers.

MOREL MUSHROOM - richly flavoured, cone shaped, wild mushroom.

MOULI - manual kitchen appliance combining a sieve and food processor.

MOUSSELINE - warm, steamed mousse usually made from vegetables, poultry or seafood.

NAM PRIK - strongly flavoured, Thai shrimp and chilli paste available from Asian supermarkets.

NICOISE OLIVES - small, lightly flavoured olives used whole in salads.

PAK CHOY - crisp, green, Asian vegetable, available from greengrocers and Asian supermarkets.

PALM SUGAR - strongly flavoured sugar made from palm sap, available from Asian supermarkets

PANINI - lightly risen, Italian peasant bread.

PEANUT OIL - cold pressed oil used in Asian cooking.

PICKLED GINGER - sweet and approachable form of ginger most frequently served with sushi, can also be used in salads and stir fries.

PINE MUSHROOM - richly flavoured, wild mushroom mainly found in Victoria during autumn.

POLENTA - coarse, corn meal used in Italian cooking, can be served either wet like a rich porridge or as a grilled bread.

PORCINI - richly flavoured, boletus mushroom from Italy, usually only seen in Australia dried or as a scented oil.

PRAWN PASTE - firm, dark paste with strong aroma used in South-East Asian cooking.

PROSCUITTO - an Italian air-dried ham, usually served thinly sliced.

QUENELLE - light, poached, seafood mousse in an oval shape made using two spoons. More commonly refers to an oval shape made with two spoons.

QUINCE PASTE - a tasty accompaniment to hard cheeses, available from delicatessans.

RADICCHIO - strong and bitter member of the lettuce family, often served cooked as well as being used in salads.

RAFT - the layer of meat, egg and spices that floats to the surface and clarifies stock when making a consomme.

RAITA - a salad of cucumber and mint served to compliment curries. Depending on the dish, other fruits or spices may be added.

RAMEKINS - round ovenware bowls with straight sides used mainly for cooking souffles and desserts.

RED WINE VINEGAR - aromatic and intensely flavoured vinegar used mainly in dressings.

REDUCTION - the boiling of liquid to intensify flavour and or viscosity.

REGGIANO PARMESAN - two-year-old, strongly flavoured, hard, grainy cheese used in Italian cooking.

REST - to set food aside for a period immediately after cooking, allows food to be served at optimum temperature and blood to be set in red meats, also refers to the gentle placing of food when garnishing a meal for serving.

RISOTTO - Italian dish usually made with arborio rice cooked in various flavoured stocks.

ROASTED SESAME OIL - intensely flavoured additive used in Asian cooking.

ROCKET - peppery flavoured lettuce, with smaller leaves that have a lighter flavour than older leaves, which can be very bitter.

ROESTI - crisp, fried potato cake.

SABLE - very short, sweet pastry used for tart shells or biscuits.

SAFFRON - fragrant spice that imparts an intense yellow colour.

SALAD ONION - SPANISH ONION, RED ONION - a lightly flavoured onion that is often served raw.

SALSA - thick, chunky sauce usually served cold.

SAMBAL OELEK - a paste made of mixed chillies and salt.

SANCHO PEPPER - Japanese lemon pepper.

SCALLION - type of spring onion with a small bulb.

SEAR - to cook the outside of food for a very short time on an intensely hot surface.

SEMOLINA - Mediterranean wheat flour used for making pasta.

SEVRUGA CAVIAR - the most affordable grade of the three, premium, genuine caviars.

SHALLOTS - a root vegetable that looks similar to garlic with a light onion flavour.

SHERRY VINEGAR - an intense, wine vinegar used mainly in salad dressings.

SHITAKE MUSHROOM - rich, meaty mushroom available either fresh or dried, if dried soak in warm water for two hours and drain before using.

SHUCK - the action of opening a shell or pod.

SICHUAN PEPPER - intense, dark red pepper used in Asian cooking.

SOBA NOODLES - Japanese buckwheat noodle often served cold in salads.

SOUR DOUGH BREAD - thick crusted, chewy, naturally leavened bread, suited to toasting or grilling.

SOUTHERN GOLD - waxy fleshed potato usually served boiled or steamed.

SPAGHETTINI - a fine spaghetti noodle.

SPAETZLI - a Germanic pasta that can be served either fried or boiled.

SQUAB PIGEON - baby pigeon, usually having a rich, game-flavoured, dark, red meat.

SQUID INK - lightly flavoured but intense colouring used in Mediterranean cooking.

STAR ANISE - aniseed flavoured spice used in Asian cooking.

STOCK SYRUP - sugar syrup, scented with vanilla, used for poaching fruits and as a component in many desserts.

TAPENADE - course pastry made mainly with black olives.

TUILE BISCUIT - fine wafer biscuit served as garnish with lightly textured desserts.

TURMERIC - member of the ginger family that imparts a bright yellow colour.

VALRHONA CHOCOLATE - a very fine, French chocolate available from a white to a very bitter dark variety.

VANILLA BEAN - the spice used to flavour the base of most custards and creams. Has a much sweeter and richer flavour than vanilla essence.

VIETNAMESE MINT - very strong, almost peppery mint, available from Asian supermarkets.

WHITE FUNGUS - SILVER FUNGUS - very lightly flavoured vegetable used mainly for texture, available dried from Asian supermarkets.

WHITE TRUFFLE - Italian, subterranean fungus with intense aroma, adds depth and richness to dishes.

WHITE TRUFFLE OIL - oil infused with white truffle, used in dressings and sauces.

WHITE WINE VINEGAR - lighter style of vinegar used in dressings, pickling and sauce reductions.

INDEX

Figures in **BOLD** indicate photographs

ALMOND ROCHERS : 142

ANCHOVY MAYONNAISE : 84

ANGLAISE : 162

AIOLI : 153

APPLE - banana stack : 134, **135**
    sauce : 102

ARMAGNAC PRUNES : 114

ASPARAGUS - poached egg & parmesan toast : 46, **47**
    tomato risotto : 58, **59**

BANANA - apple stack : 134, **135**
    ice cream : 160

BEARNAISE SAUCE : 110

BEEF - Bordelaise sauce : 106, **107**
    lemon peppered salad : 22, **23**
    chilli & black bean jus : 39
    jus : 150
    veal stock : 148
    steak & kidney pie : 108
    Bearnaise sauce : 110, **111**

BEETROOT RELISH : 109

BERRIES - brandy snap : 126, **127**

BLACK TRUFFLE - dressing : 86
    sauce : 96

BORDELAISE SAUCE : 152

BRAINS - tartlet : 90, **91**

BRANDY SNAPS : 126, **127**

BREAD AND BUTTER CUSTARD : 136, **137**

BROTH - mushroom : 83
    seafood and lemongrass : 16, **17**

BROWNIE - chocolate : 132, **133**

BUGS - lemongrass broth : 16, **17**
    nam prik sauce : 30, **31**
    linguine with herb oil : 64, **65**

CABBAGE - creamed : 95

CALAMARI - spaghettini & tapenade : 66

CAPSICUM JAM : 158

CARAMEL SAUCE : 134

CAVIAR - scrambled egg & smoked salmon : 88, **89**

CHEESE - selection and serving : 144, **145**

CHERMOULAH : 67

CHERRIES - chocolate sorbet : 120

CHEVRE - see GOAT'S CHEESE

CHICKEN - stock : 148
    risotto salad : 50, **51**
    borlotti beans & sausage : 74, **75**
    leek mousseline & morels : 96, **97**
    jus : 151

CHILLI - & black bean jus : 39
    dressing : 22
    namprik : 155

CHOCOLATE DARK - rochers : 142
    truffles : 142
    tart : 130, **131**
    brownie : 132, **133**
    sorbet : 120
    sauce : 132
    souffle : 118, **119**

CHOCOLATE WHITE - creme brulee : 116,
    ice cream : 161

COCONUT - dressing : 20
    roast ice cream : 161

CONFIT - onion : 158

CONSOMME - peking duck : 18

CORN SALSA : 26

COS - rocket with anchovy mayonnaise : 84, **85**

COURT BOUILLON : 149

COUS COUS : 54

CREAMED - cabbage : 95

CREME ANGLAISE : 162

CREME BRULEE - vanilla : 114, **115**
    white chocolate : 116

CREPES - lemon : 128, **129**

CUTTLEFISH - lemongrass broth : 16, **17**
    linguine : 32
    Moroccan spiced : 54, **55**

DEMI GLACE : 149

DRUNKEN FRUIT : 163
    pudding : 138, **139**

DUCK - Peking consomme : 18
    Peking stock : 149
    Peking barbecued : 42, **43**
    Peking sauce : 151

EGGS - poached : 157, 46, **47**
    scrambled with smoked salmon : 88, **89**

FISH - fragrant steamed : 38
    ocean trout cured : 24
    tuna nicoise : 53
    saffron beurre blanc : 94
    see also SALMON

FOIE GRAS - butter : 152

GARLIC - roast : 159
    onion soup : 82
    bruschetta : 52

GAZPACHO : 52

GNOCCHI - with prawn & tomato : 68, **69**

GOAT'S CHEESE - stack : 48, **49**

GUINEA FOWL - creamed cabbage : 95

HAZELNUT & ORANGE - sable : 141

HERB OIL : 153

ICE CREAM - vanilla : 160
    banana : 160
    black sambucca : 160
    lemon myrtle : 160
    red wine : 161
    roast coconut : 161
    white chocolate : 161

KIDNEYS - bacon & seeded mustard : 92, **93**
    steak pie : 108

LAMB - red curry : 40, **41**
    nicoise vegetables : 72, **73**
    brains tartlet : 90, **91**
    parsnip mash & peas : 104, **105**
    jus : 150

LEEK MOUSSELINE : 158

LEMON - crepes : 128, **129**
    souffle : 117
    syrup : 128

LEMON MYRTLE - ice cream : 160

LEMONGRASS - broth : 16, **17**
    poached prawn salad : 20, **21**

LIVER - braised radicchio : 70, **71**

MADEIRA SAUCE : 152

MANGO - tart : 124, **125**

MASHED POTATO : 157

MAYONNAISE - Asian spice : 24
    base : 153

MOREL MUSHROOM - chicken & leek : 96

MORETON BAY BUGS - see BUGS

MUDCRAB - Jack's omelette : 28, **29**

MUSHROOM - risotto : 62, **63**
    broth : 83
    omelette : 87

MUSSELS - saffron risotto : 60, **61**

MUSTARD SAUCE : 151

NAM PRIK SAUCE : 155

NICOISE SALAD : 53

NICOISE VEGETABLES : 72

OCEAN TROUT - Asian spice cured : 24

OMELETTE - Jack's mudcrab : 28, **29**
    mushroom : 87

ONION - confit : 158
    garlic soup : 82

OYSTERS - red wine vinegar sauce : 80, **81**

PARMESAN BRIOCHE : 156

PASSIONFRUIT SYRUP : 124

PARSNIP MASH : 104

PEACH - raspberry trifle : 121

PEARS - poached red wine : 122, **123**

PEKING DUCK - see DUCK

PIGEON - see SQUAB PIGEON

POACHED EGGS : 157
    and asparagus : 46, **47**

POLENTA : 157
    with veal shanks : 76, **77**

PORK - roast suckling : 102, **103**

POTATO MASH : 157

PRAWNS - lemongrass broth : 16, **17**
    lemongrass poached salad : 20, **21**
    grilled yellow curry : 25
    & gnocchi in tomato sauce : 68, **69**

PRUNES - Armagnac : 114

PUDDING - drunken fruit : 138, **139**
    bread & butter : 136, **137**

PUFF PASTRY : 108

PUMPKIN - Thai soup : 19

QUAIL - marinated salad : 33
    yellow curry sauce : 34, **35**

RADICCHIO - braised : 70

RAITA : 34

RASPBERRY - puree : 162
    trifle : 121
    white chocolate brulee : 116

RED CURRY PASTE : 40

RED WINE - ice cream : 161
    poached pear : 122, **123**

RED WINE VINEGAR - dressing : 53
    dipping sauce : 80

RISOTTO - tomato & asparagus : 58, **59**
    chicken salad : 50, **51**
    salad of squid ink & scallops : 57
    mushroom : 62, **63**
    mussel with saffron : 60, **61**

ROAST GARLIC : 159
    & onion soup : 82

ROCHERS - almond : 142

ROCKET - cos salad with anchovy mayonnaise : 84, **85**

ROESTI : 100, **101**

SABLE PASTRY - plain : 163
    hazelnut & orange : 141

SAFFRON - risotto : 60, **61**
    beurre blanc : 94

SALMON - soy & lime butter : 36, **37**
    chermoulah crusted : 67
    smoked with scrambled eggs : 88, **89**

SAMBUCCA - ice cream : 160

SAUTERNE CAKE - summer fruits : 140

SCALLOPS - corn salsa : 26, **27**
    lemongrass broth : 16, **17**
    squid ink risotto : 57
    white truffle butter : 56

SCRAMBLED EGGS - smoked salmon & caviar : 88, **89**

SHALLOTS - roast : 159

SHORT PASTRY : 90

SHORTBREAD : 141

SMOKED SALMON - scrambled eggs & caviar : 88, **89**

SOFT POLENTA : 157

SORBET - chocolate : 120

SOUFFLE - chocolate : 118, **119**
    lemon : 117

SOY & LIME BUTTER : 36

SPAETZLI : 156

SQUAB PIGEON - foie gras butter : 98, **99**

SQUID INK - pasta : 64, **65**
    risotto : 57

STOCK SYRUP : 162

TAPENADE : 66

TART - mango : 124, **125**
    chocolate : 130, **131**

TARTLET - lamb's brains : 90, **91**

TOMATO - risotto : 58, **59**
    sauce : 68

TRIFLE - peach & raspberry : 121

TRUFFLE - see WHITE, BLACK and CHOCOLATE

TUILE BISCUITS : 163

TUNA - nicoise salad : 53

VANILLA BEAN - anglaise : 162
    brulee : 114, **115**
    ice cream : 160

VEAL - shanks & soft polenta : 76, **77**
    wild mushrooms : 100, **101**
    kidneys & mustard sauce : 92, **93**
    stock : 148

VENISON - beetroot relish : 109
    jus : 150

VERMICELLI - salad : 33

WALNUT OIL - truffle dressing : 86

WHITE TRUFFLE - butter : 56

YABBIES - truffle & walnut oil dressing : 86

YELLOW CURRY - dressing : 25
    oil : 154

LIST OF RECIPE PHOTOGRAPHS

- APPLE AND BANANA STACK: 135
- BITTER SWEET CHOCOLATE TART WITH CITRUS SALAD: 131
- BLACK LIP MUSSELS WITH SAFFRON RISOTTO: 61
- BRAISED VEAL SHANKS WITH SOFT POLENTA: 77
- BRANDY SNAPS WITH SUMMER BERRIES: 127
- BREAD AND BUTTER CUSTARD: 137
- BREAST OF CHICKEN WITH LEEK MOUSSELINE & MOREL MUSHROOMS: 97
- CHAR-GRILLED ASPARAGUS ON TOMATO RISOTTO: 59
- CHEESE: 145
- CHICKEN BREAST WITH BORLOTTI BEANS AND TUSCAN SAUSAGE: 75
- CHOCOLATE BROWNIE WITH ROAST COCONUT ICE CREAM: 133
- CHOCOLATE SOUFFLE WITH WHITE CHOCOLATE ICE CREAM: 119
- DRUNKEN FRUIT STEAMED PUDDING: 139
- FILLET OF BEEF WITH BORDELAISE SAUCE: 107
- FRESHLY SHUCKED OYSTERS WITH RED WINE VINEGAR DIPPING SAUCE: 81
- GNOCCHI & PRAWNS IN TOMATO SAUCE: 69
- GRILLED QUAIL ON YELLOW CURRY SAUCE WITH RAITA: 35
- JACK'S MUDCRAB OMELETTE: 29
- LAMB WITH NICOISE VEGETABLES: 73
- LEMON CREPES WITH BLACK SAMBUCCA ICE CREAM: 129
- LEMON PEPPERED BEEF SALAD WITH CHILLI DRESSING: 23
- LOIN OF LAMB WITH GARDEN PEAS AND PARSNIP MASH: 105
- MANGO TART & LIME CREAM: 125
- MEDITERRANEAN GOAT'S CHEESE STACK: 49
- MILK FED VEAL ON ROESTI WITH WILD MUSHROOMS: 101
- MORETON BAY BUGS ON LINGUINE WITH HERB OIL: 65
- MORETON BAY BUGS WITH NAM PRIK SAUCE: 31
- MOROCCAN SPICED CUTTLEFISH WITH FRUITY COUS COUS: 55
- PEKING STYLE BARBECUED DUCK: 43
- RACK OF SUCKLING PORK WITH ROAST VEGETABLES: 103
- RED CURRY LAMB FILLETS: 41
- RED WINE POACHED PEARS WITH RED WINE ICE CREAM: 123
- RIB OF BEEF WITH BEARNAISE SAUCE: 111
- RISOTTO OF WILD AND FIELD MUSHROOMS: 63
- RISOTTO SALAD WITH CHICKEN TENDERLOINS: 51
- ROCKET AND COS SALAD WITH ANCHOVY MAYONNAISE: 85
- SALAD OF LEMONGRASS POACHED PRAWNS & COCONUT DRESSING: 21
- SCRAMBLED EGGS AND SMOKED SALMON WITH CAVIAR: 89
- SEAFOOD AND LEMONGRASS BROTH: 18
- SEARED CALVE'S LIVER ON BRAISED RADICCHIO: 71
- SEARED SCALLOPS WITH CORN SALSA: 27
- SEARED VEAL KIDNEYS WITH BACON AND SEEDED MUSTARD: 93
- SPICED SALMON FILLET WITH SOY & LIME BUTTER: 37
- SQUAB PIGEON WITH FOIE GRAS BUTTER: 99
- STEAMED ASPARAGUS WITH POACHED EGG AND PARMESAN TOAST: 47
- TARTLET OF LAMB'S BRAINS ON ONION CONFIT: 91
- VANILLA BEAN CREME BRULEE WITH ARMAGNAC PRUNES: 115

THANK - YOU

Most people in the hospitality industry dream of the day they own their own restaurant. When you own that restaurant, the dreams grow and one of the ambitions becomes writing a book. Achieving these dreams takes many, many people.

The ones putting up with the most and deserving the greatest thanks are our wives and families. Often they only see us for very short periods in the mornings or on days off (if we're not dropping into the restaurant, doing odd jobs for the restaurant, nothing breaks down and no-one gets sick or chops off a finger).

Thanks to all our staff at the restaurant. They see more of us than our family, but also have to put up with more from us. They start work early, then make up for it by finishing late. Days off are never certain and last minute changes are the rule rather than the exception.

Thank-you to the all people who have dined at the restaurant during the last eight years and tasted how our food has evolved. We look forward to seeing many more patrons in the years to come. Thanks also to the numerous suppliers constantly trying to meet our demands for premium produce.

When the people at The Studio first told us it was "not that hard to publish your own book", we believed them ... thanks for fibbing.

So many people have put in a lot of hard work to cook up this book. Here are a few of them:

The book's art director, George, who kept us all on track to meet the publishing schedule (and mainly got his own way), as well as Mark, Darryl, Michelle, Luke, Matthew and everyone else from The Studio at Delta Technology who helped turn our restaurant into a book.

Peter Budd for his images; Myra Givan for making sure we had our "i"s dotted and our "t"s crossed; and of course Glyn Davies, Caroline Jones, Gavin Evans, Nathan Micallef, David Holdsworth, Conal Reilly, Frank Flynn, Adam Sing, Kiri Binning, Tony Judd and Narelle Wilshot at the restaurant.

The photograph on the following page shows some of these talented contributors.

And thanks again, to our wives Jenny and Paula ... we'll be home soon, honest.

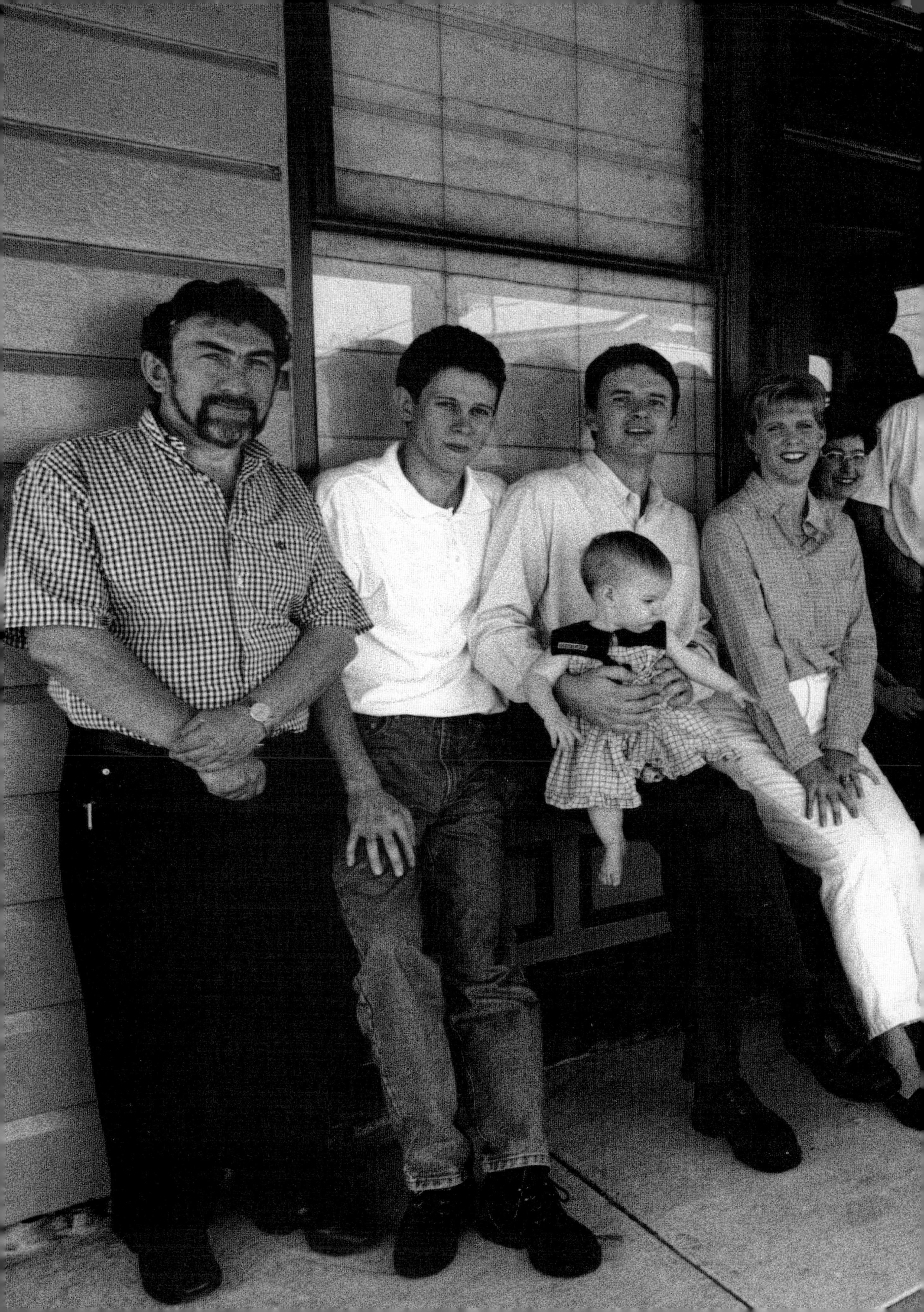